CANOEING

Look for these other Trailside® Series Guides:

Bicycling: Touring and Mountain Bike Basics
Cross-Country Skiing: A Complete Guide
Fly Fishing: A Trailside Guide
Hiking & Backpacking: A Complete Guide
Kayaking: Whitewater and Touring Basics
Winter Adventure: A Complete Guide to Winter Sports

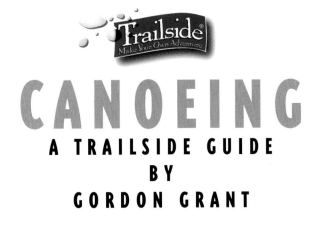

CANOEING
A TRAILSIDE GUIDE
BY
GORDON GRANT

Illustrations by Ron Hildebrand

A TRAILSIDE SERIES GUIDE

W. W. NORTON & COMPANY

NEW YORK   LONDON

Copyright © 1997 by New Media, Incorporated
All rights reserved
Printed in Hong Kong

First Edition

The text of this book is composed in Bodoni Book with the display set in Triplex
Page composition by Tina Christensen
Color separations and prepress by Bergman Graphics, Incorporated
Manufacturing by South China Printing Co. Ltd.
Illustrations by Ron Hildebrand

Book design by Bill Harvey

Library of Congress Cataloging-in-Publication Data

Grant, Gordon 1955—
Canoeing: a trailside guide / by Gordon Grant;
illustrations by Ron Hildebrand
p.   cm. — (A Trailside series guide)
Includes bibliographical references and index.
1. Canoes and canoeing. 2. Canoes and canoeing — Safety measures.
3. Canoes and canoeing — Equipment and supplies. 4. Rafting (Sports)
I. Title. II. Series.
GV783.G73   1997   797.1'22—dc20   96-2151 CIP

ISBN 0-393-31489-8

W. W. Norton & Company, Inc., 500 Fifth Avenue, New York, N. Y. 10110
http://www.wwnorton.com
W. W. Norton & Company Ltd., 10 Coptic Street, London WC1A 1PU

1 2 3 4 5 6 7 8 9 0

CONTENTS

INTRODUCTION

There is music on the waters, and for millennia humankind has developed ways to harmonize with it: Just watch kids in endless play at the beach or local swimming hole; hikers mesmerized beneath the spray of a great falls; the hanging calligraphy of the fly-fisher's roll cast catching the light; a surfer executing a precise carving bottom turn in the thundering hollow of an ocean wave. Or the canoeist, moving down long rapids in complete control, playing the waves, stopping in the eddies where the trout feed, at home amidst all the power.

For their practitioners, it is even hard to call these activities sports. Rather they are part of an older dance with the oldest partner of all. They define who you are. They take only a few simple tools, a few refined movements that require a short time to learn and a lifetime to master, and a willingness to be a joyful apprentice to your craft for the remainder of your days.

This is a book about one of those passions — canoeing on lake, river, and white water. The canoe was developed in response to the needs of Native peoples of North America several thousand years ago. Like the flowing curve of the Viking ship or the narrow grace of the Greenland kayak, there is a timeless appeal to the shape of the canoe: a boat small enough to be carried, yet capable of carrying much; upturned ends to deflect the waters; narrow and straight enough to carry its speed, yet with a graceful curve of hull that allows quick turns. The canoe's shape is a perfect design that still inspires fascination.

Most Americans have spent some time, somewhere, in a canoe. It is impossible to estimate how many canoes are put to use every year in summer camps, canoe liveries, and by private owners across the continent. In fact, if you were to ask, a surprising number of people would say they know how to canoe, or at least "used to do it a lot." What most are describing is the basic first stage of canoeing on lakes: sitting up on the seats with knees crisping in the sun, switching sides vigorously with a paddle clutched, clublike, in their hands, the boat veering back and forth. It is simple, it is accessible to millions, and it is an enjoyable end in itself. It is also not what I will share in this book.

This book is for the person who wants to experience the pleasure that comes from moving a canoe in good control, whether on a lake or down swift rivers or whitewater rapids. On lakes, the gratification comes from efficient control of the craft once the paddler is competent in a few strokes; then it is just a matter of getting out there and using the canoe as a vehicle for quiet exploration. Once water starts to move downhill, it gathers force and power and is less tolerant of mistakes. But the laws it obeys are simple, as are the strokes needed by the canoeist.

———————————————

❝ This music crept by me upon the waters,
Allaying both their fury and my passion
With its sweet air; thence I have follow'd it,
Or it hath drawn me rather. But 'tis gone.
No, it begins again. ❞

Shakespeare, *The Tempest*

———————————————

I have been paddling canoes on lakes and rivers for more than 25 years. From the very start, my learning of the sport has been shaped by excellent, friendly, and highly sequential instruction — instruction that has led to my experiences being almost wholly joyous ones. I have paddled rivers — some of considerable difficulty — on several continents, but I have few horror stories to tell because I have almost always been in control of myself and my canoe, as I was taught. I've had my share of flips, swims, adventures, and misadventures, but owing to the training I received, they have all been manageable. It is that sequence of training that I want to share with you.

Most of my canoeing has been done as student and instructor at two institutions in the mountains of North Carolina: Camp Mondamin and the Nantahala

Outdoor Center. At Mondamin, I learned the sport in a program that is now in its 75th year, one that has introduced thousands of young people to running white water with grace and style. Mondamin has the time — a six-week summer session — to insist that its canoeists learn solid competence in each phase of boat control before they move on to more difficult rivers. Once

on white water, the camp canoeists refine their skills by "working" small rapids, isolating specific moves, and repeating them as a gymnast would a routine, until the reactions needed for white water are so ingrained that the kids can be counted on to execute them in any situation.

After learning the sport at Mondamin, I followed John Burton, a former counselor there and 1972 Olympic Team member, to the newly established Nantahala Outdoor Center (NOC), where he was to become director and later president. The NOC has become internationally recognized for its excellence in whitewater instruction. In the more than 20 years since its founding by Payson and Aurelia Kennedy, it has become the largest school of canoe and kayak instruction in North America and has consistently attracted the foremost practitioners of the sport. Among them are key influences on my paddling: Bunny Johns, the current president of NOC and an early developer of American Canoe Association instructor standards; Les Bechdel, a many-time U.S. Team member and innovator in river rescue techniques; and Kent Ford, another U.S. Team member who has gone on to make a series of excellent instructional videos.

At Mondamin, I discovered that skill and judgment, not equipment, are the real source of safety on the river, and I learned a highly functional progression of teaching strokes to develop those skills. At the NOC, I learned to compress instructional tips into a compact sequence that can be taught over a shorter time. In this book, I am endeavoring to blend those experiences into an instructional pattern useful for the novice canoeist who needs a map into a new territory of skills.

I don't want to attempt too much: I want readers to focus on each step in the basics of building up competence to a moderate level of white water in under a month of practice and experimentation. If this book helps more people develop their canoeing skills with a sense of the joy of mastering each step, then it will have served its purpose well. Nothing can match the experience of learning a sport with a first-rate instructor at your side, but for those of you who cannot get away for an extended period, I have tried to incorporate the same principles of learning and skills building I have used in classes on-stream.

Perfecting those skills takes much longer. That is the fun of it. This book focuses on skills; it does not claim to cover all the many delightful special aspects of canoeing, such as sailing, poling, wilderness expeditions, extreme white water, and racing. If you are interested in those activities, a sources section at the end of the book will help you further your inquiries.

This book is set up to help you through a period of pleasurable apprenticeship. It begins with the assumption that you will be aiming for some quick results in paddling canoes, first on quiet water and then, if you choose, on moving and white water, either alone or with a partner in your boat. In each chapter, you'll get some guidance on the type of equipment you will need for the kind of boating you'll be doing. The opening chapters center on the simple sets of strokes required to control the boat. Subsequent chapters show you how to apply those strokes on moving water and give you exercises for paddling on easy rapids that will prepare you with much better control in larger ones.

From start to finish, I share the safety lessons I've learned over 25 years, lessons that have kept the risks that are part of this sport at an acceptably low level. Intelligently managing risk is one of the beauties of canoeing. That is why it is such a great sport to teach young people, as I am teaching my children, as I hope you will teach yours.

— *Gordon Grant*

GEARING UP:
THE BASICS

L et's go canoeing! The boats are affordable, the strokes to learn are few, and there are navigable bodies of water close to every American. While the rest of our citizens are sweltering in the cities, watching TV, and pining for vacations they can't afford, *we* will be out on the water, acquiring skills that will make it possible for us to explore the entire continent and beyond. There is a creek, a lake, or a river not 10 miles from your home. You don't need a powerboat that costs a second mortgage; you don't need a trailer or a boat ramp to winch the thing into and out of the water. All you need is a canoe and a paddle and a life jacket.

GEARING UP

If you become addicted to canoeing, you will spend many satisfying hours poring over the books, magazines, and catalogues that lovingly describe all the exciting places you can go and all the great stuff you can buy to make canoeing ever more enjoyable. At this point, however, you simply want to learn to canoe. To begin, all you need are a canoe that will handle lakes and moderate white water, a paddle to propel it, and a life jacket to keep you buoyant when the inevitable spills occur.

First Canoe

For your first canoe, I recommend a

tough plastic — or possibly aluminum — model from 15 to 17 feet long. It will look just like what you imagine a canoe *should* look like: a slender boat about 3 feet wide amidships, with sides that take long, symmetrical, tapering curves to either end. Small decks end in identical bow and stern, upturned ends recurved slightly back toward the center of the boat. This is simplicity itself — the purest example of form following function — and you can't go too far wrong, provided you keep a few points in mind.

Avoid models with a deep keel (a ridge of material running down the length of the

Anatomy of a Canoe

Gunwale

Bow Deck

EXPLORER

exterior of the boat's hull that helps keep it on a straight course). You'll find small keels on the ubiquitous Grumman aluminum and Coleman plastic canoes found at so many

liveries and canoe rental places; these are OK. Ideally, though, the hull of your first canoe should be smooth to allow easy turning. Keeping it going straight? Well, you'll learn that soon enough.

The main thing to remember is that nearly any canoe will do to get you started in this sport.

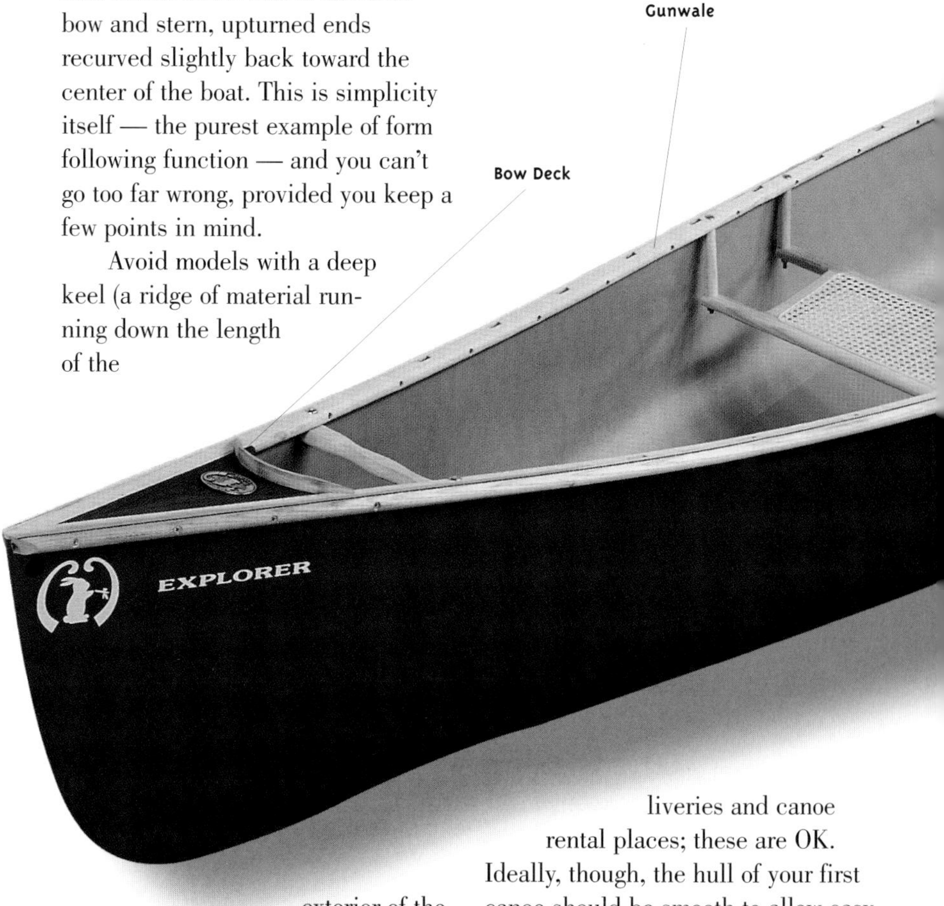

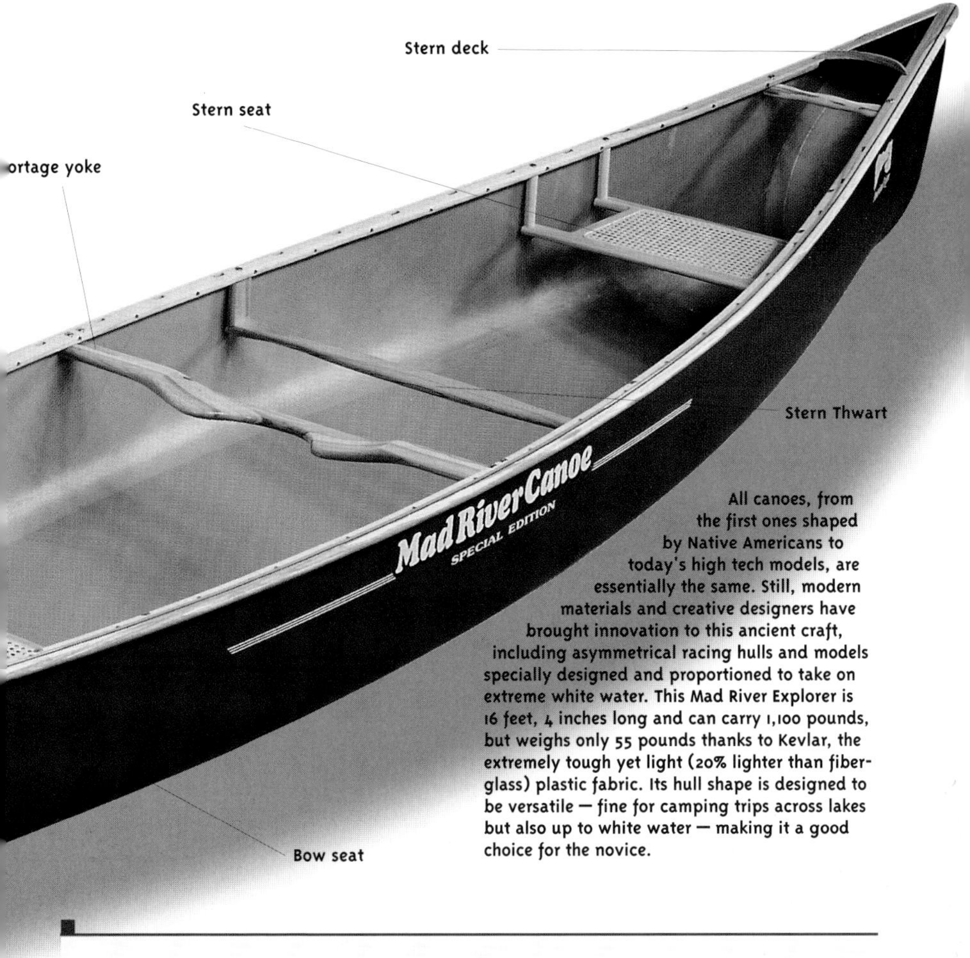

Stern deck

Stern seat

ortage yoke

Stern Thwart

Mad River Canoe
SPECIAL EDITION

All canoes, from the first ones shaped by Native Americans to today's high tech models, are essentially the same. Still, modern materials and creative designers have brought innovation to this ancient craft, including asymmetrical racing hulls and models specially designed and proportioned to take on extreme white water. This Mad River Explorer is 16 feet, 4 inches long and can carry 1,100 pounds, but weighs only 55 pounds thanks to Kevlar, the extremely tough yet light (20% lighter than fiberglass) plastic fabric. Its hull shape is designed to be versatile — fine for camping trips across lakes but also up to white water — making it a good choice for the novice.

Bow seat

GEAR TALK

WILL IT SINK?

All modern canoes float, even when swamped, either because of the natural buoyancy of their hulls (wood or plastic laminated to layers of aircelled foam) or because the makers have sealed flotation compartments into the boat along the gunwales and under the seats and decks (aluminum and fiberglass models). When swamped, however, a canoe floats right at the water's surface level, with only the upturned bow and stern above water. For white water, additional flotation is required, which we will discuss in Chapter 6.

There are few more satisfying expressions of craftsmanship than that of a classic wooden canoe. This one, on Lower Ausable Lake in New York State's Adirondack Mountains, is headed off into classic canoe country.

white water. While lake paddles generally are longer than whitewater ones, a good rough rule is that, when standing beside a paddle with its blade tip on the ground, its grip should reach somewhere between your chin and your nose.

Most modern all-purpose paddles and almost all whitewater ones have somewhat squared-off blades and T-shaped grips to give paddlers greater dexterity and control. Old-fashioned "beavertail" paddles have longer, nar-

The Paddle

Paddles come in a variety of blade shapes and grip styles. Let's look at the parts of a standard paddle that could be used on either a lake or rower, more rounded blades and a wider, rounded grip. Either type is fine for our first sessions on flat water, although a T-grip model is best in most situations.

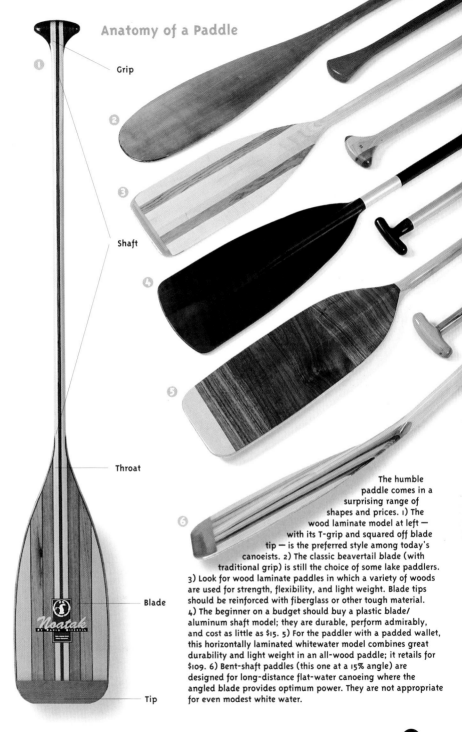

Anatomy of a Paddle

Grip

Shaft

Throat

Blade

Tip

The humble paddle comes in a surprising range of shapes and prices. 1) The wood laminate model at left — with its T-grip and squared off blade tip — is the preferred style among today's canoeists. 2) The classic beavertail blade (with traditional grip) is still the choice of some lake paddlers. 3) Look for wood laminate paddles in which a variety of woods are used for strength, flexibility, and light weight. Blade tips should be reinforced with fiberglass or other tough material. 4) The beginner on a budget should buy a plastic blade/ aluminum shaft model; they are durable, perform admirably, and cost as little as $15. 5) For the paddler with a padded wallet, this horizontally laminated whitewater model combines great durability and light weight in an all-wood paddle; it retails for $109. 6) Bent-shaft paddles (this one at a 15% angle) are designed for long-distance flat-water canoeing where the angled blade provides optimum power. They are not appropriate for even modest white water.

PFDs (personal flotation devices) are required gear for all safety-conscious boaters, but particularly whitewater canoeists and kayakers. Many styles are available, but stick with U.S. Coast Guard-approved Type III models with zip fronts. Be sure to find the right fit for maximum safety and comfort; any chafing at your arms or shoulders will quickly become annoying or even unbearable.

Life Jacket (PFD)

I am a strong believer in life jackets, nowadays called PFDs (personal flotation devices). They provide buoyancy and warmth in case of a spill, allow you to use your energy to collect your wits and your gear and to resolve potentially nasty situations, and are indispensable in white water. In short, PFDs make canoeing safer. Most states require that you carry one PFD for each person aboard your boat. Many states go further, requiring that each person wear a properly fitted and fastened PFD. Properly fitted means that once the jacket is zipped, slipped, or clipped on and all the adjustments have been made secure, it fits snugly enough that it cannot be pulled up to your ears. If it can, it is too loose and needs to be readjusted or a smaller jacket size selected.

Only Coast Guard-approved Type III (vest type) jackets are appropriate for lake and whitewater use. Be sure to buy a PFD specifically designed for paddling; water-skiing models are too stiff and are cut with insufficient arm room for the motions of paddling.

That said, I'd like to offer a qualification. Canoeing is a sport where the least possible gear affords the most possible pleasure; there are times when I do not wear a life jacket, and I enjoy those times very much. It's the acquisition of *skills*, not equipment, that really counts. A skilled paddler who is a strong swimmer may well be safer than an unskilled paddler convinced of his invulnerability by a ton of expensive gear.

If you are a strong swimmer, you'll delight occasionally in taking your canoe to a quiet body of water and exploring without wearing your life jacket. The feel of moving the boat through the water unencumbered is wonderful. Granted, letters to the editors of boating magazines roundly denounce pictures of people happily paddling across lakes without wearing their PFDs, and the editors are obliged to make diplomatic statements in response. But risk cannot be removed from living.

Sports that involve risk — and almost all do — give their partici-

The canoe is everyman's recreational vessel, a versatile craft that can turn with ease from one pleasurable pursuit to another, including bass fishing with your golden retriever on a local lake.

pants satisfaction in part by providing opportunities to take calculated risks. If you are a strong swimmer and are paddling on flat

That's your choice, and the consequences of a flip are yours. Make your decision wisely, not based on vanity, the desire for the perfect tan, or what your friends might say. If you are making a long, open-water crossing, are wearing bulky clothing that would hinder swimming, or are in water with any current, you must, of course, wear your PFD.

Use common sense and, when in doubt, err on the side of caution. I always have my PFD with me, and it is seldom not on

Like no other vehicle, the canoe is adapted to taking you quietly and efficiently deep into wild places, as here, on the Rio Grande, in the arid, rugged Big Bend National Park, in southwest Texas.

water close to shore, it may be reasonable to you to paddle without wearing the PFD in your boat. and properly fastened. But the choice to take it off is mine, and I exercise it.

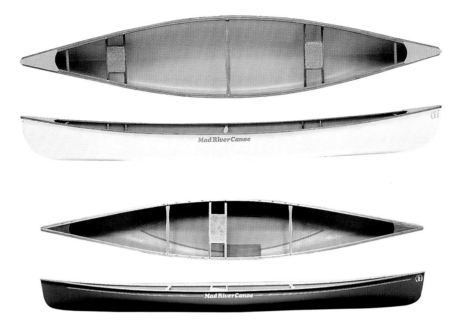

Tandem vs. Solo: Note the difference in seat and thwart placement as well as hull profile between the tandem (2-person) canoe at top and the solo model at bottom. Note also that the center thwart of the tandem canoe is positioned such that, when seated facing the stern, this craft may also be paddled solo. The tandem canoe is made of Royalex molded plastic, is 16 feet long, and weighs 72 pounds; the solo model, of Kevlar, is 15 feet, 8 inches long and weighs 30 pounds.

PURCHASING GEAR — TWO PATHS
The Tightwad

If Thoreau's philosophy of simplicity is your chosen path, you are unsure you really want to sink a lot of money into a new sport, or money is just plain tight, consider the following:

Rent a canoe for a day or so from a livery or outfitter in your area if you're really uncertain about this new pursuit. Cost is usually about $20 to $40 a day and should include paddles and PFDs for both paddlers. What could be simpler or more frugal? When you are ready to buy, here is the rock-bottom way to get started.

CANOE. You're searching for an unadorned workhorse, a used general-purpose canoe. You can find what you want advertised in the local paper, paddling-club newsletters, or at your local canoeing outfitter, who has accepted used boats as trade-ins from customers buying newer models. Or inquire at a local livery; whenever one upgrades its fleet, it sells off old canoes.

Look for an old Grumman aluminum or a well-maintained Royalex plastic model by Dagger, Mad River, Mohawk, or Old Town. Stay away from old fiberglass boats: They get brittle with age. Old wooden canoes may require restoration — for some folks, a satisfying end in itself — but do you want to start paddling this year? A decent used canoe will set you back $300 to $500.

PADDLE. Unless you find a real steal in a used paddle, go with a new one from Carlisle or Mohawk. Many manufacturers offer a "price point" paddle of questionable quality, but Carlisle and Mohawk offer cheap ones that really do hold up to abuse and feel decent in the water. Their basic paddles, with plastic-coated aluminum shafts and plastic blades, cost less than $15 and are fine for lake work. If you plan to paddle white water, go with a beefier version, such as the Carlisle Commercial, for about $25. This paddle is a marvel of efficiency and pleasing feel for such a low price.

PFD. Only a few manufacturers are licensed to make Coast Guard-approved PFDs in the United States. Extrasport, Mad River, Perception, and Stohlquist all make fine products. Their basic Type IIIs range from $50 to $70. Don't shortcut on this item: If you buy a bargain-bin special from the local MegaMart, your chafed arms will remind you of your parsimony for days. Even worse, the loose fit of the cheap jackets means they come off easily, a serious flaw.

OTHER GEAR. Nothing you don't already have: shorts, sunscreen, old sneakers, and a hat. If you purchased a boat with no outfitting included, you'll need knee pads to be comfortable in the kneeling position that I recommend. Standard bike, basketball, and wrestling ones cost about $8. Some of the cushier foam jobs used by gardeners and bricklayers go for $15, but they can be bulky and awkward to walk around in.

You can avoid shelling out several hundred dollars on a fancy roof rack to transport your boat to the water's edge by buying foam blocks ($10 for a set) that slip onto the boat's gunwales, padding them from the roof of your car (see "Roof Racks," page 31).

Total start-up cost for the follower of Thoreau, seeker of inner peace and bargains: $375 to $600. For the countless pleasurable adventures the modest outlay will bring you, this has to be one of the best recreational deals in America.

The Champion of Craftsmanship

You love well-made outdoor gear and are willing to pay for it. Well-crafted forms in wood, metal, or other materials shaped by the demands of function bring you lasting enjoyment as you put them to use in the field. People with your appreciation for quality allow a number of smaller companies building specialized boats and equipment to survive. Good job. You are helping perpetuate an art form.

CANOE. If you plan on sticking to lakes and you are drawn to the tradition of canoeing, a wooden boat is an obvious choice. There are still a number of companies producing elegant woodstrip canoes that will be heirlooms for several generations beyond you. Old Town, Island Falls Canoes, McCurdy and Reed, and individual boatbuilders like Kevin Martin all produce exquisite canoes that run anywhere from $1,800 to $3,500.

It is a rare individual who subjects wooden canoes to the abuses of white water. If you want a whitewater boat that is made of tough modern materials but also boasts some nice touches of craftsmanship, look to companies such as Dagger Canoe and Mad River Canoe, which have a wide variety of Royalex models with options packages that include wooden gunwales and cane seats in boats ranging from $900 to $1,500.

Finally, for the lightest-weight boats for flat or white water, you will want one of the Kevlar composite hulls. Not to be confused with fiberglass, these are molded plastic laminates that are stiff, light, strong — and expensive. Long-distance lake trippers or those who want the highest performance in white water should consider these designs, available from Millbrook Boats, Mad River Canoe, Swift Canoe, and others for from $1,000 to $2,000.

PADDLE. Wood warms the heart of the traditionalist, and interestingly, it is preferred by many whitewater canoeists as well as lake trippers. Beautiful custom wood paddles are made by many small shops, foremost among them being Mitchell, Silver Creek, and Cricket, but they are also available from Mad River, Grey Owl, Great Canadian, and others.

For the lightest weight and stiffness, many paddlers are going to synthetic paddles by Perception, Werner, and Grasse River Boatworks, among others. The cost of a good wood or synthetic canoe paddle ranges from $80 to $300.

PFD. Here, as I mentioned above, the budget hunter and the connoisseur

venience, but there isn't much room to spend more money on a jacket, nor is there need. OTHER GEAR. Ah, now we get into the area that follows an infinite curve upward. There is all manner of extra gear out there designed to make your life in a canoe more comfortable, stylish, and convenient. Clothing by L.L. Bean, The North Face, Patagonia, and other outfitters is continuously being refined and improved with new designs and materials. My advice on these

To the water's edge: a pair of canoeists set off in a sturdy aluminum boat, choice of many canoe liveries. Note that the stern paddler has gotten in first; it's easiest for the bow paddler to push off from shore and gingerly get into position just behind the bow deck.

share the same gear. All the manufacturers listed — Extrasport, Stohlquist, Headwaters, and Perception — make excellent PFDs ranging from $50 to $150. The more expensive jackets have some features for whitewater needs or pockets for con-

is to read the catalogs and magazine product reviews. Buy what brings you pleasure. But remember, all you need for a good day on the lake are a pair of shorts and shoes that you don't mind getting wet. If you want specialized clothing for paddling, what you

Canoe campers on portage: on relatively short carries, walking beside the upright canoe and holding it by the bow and stern deck plates is an easy way for two people with one canoe to get it from one lake to another.

will find from all these manufacturers is stuff that either repels water or, when wet, dries quickly. We'll get into more detail on garments specially designed for whitewater canoeing in Chapter 7 (see page 125).

Total start-up cost for the connoisseur of quality: $1,600 to $4,000. As you can see, even the top end of canoeing does not compare with the many thousands of dollars spent on some other sports. Nor are there greens fees and club dues to the thousands of North American lakes and rivers. Canoeing and the adventures it makes possible are within the range of most of us.

What of the average person, whose budget lies between hard-core frugality and wanton pursuit of artistry and quality? This person can expect to pay $800 to $1,200 to get started in canoeing. Figure on the low end of the range if you plan to stick to flat water and on the upper end if you aim for white water and its additional safety gear.

TO THE WATER'S EDGE

Unless you have the luxury of a personal canoe caddie to transport your boat to and from the water's edge, you will have to learn to hump the thing around yourself and to do so safely. Although two people are best for that job, I'll explain how to do the same thing solo without throwing your back out (see "Loading and Unloading Alone," page 30). The average canoe weighs between 60 and 80 pounds. Since, for your first lake session, you have gone to a pal's house to borrow her boat and gear, you must get the canoe from behind the house, where it is resting upside down, and heft it up onto the car racks. Here's how two people would do just that.

Standard Carry

Roll the boat over. Grab it under its bow and stern deck plates; most models have

The standard tandem carry: the upright canoe is carried on opposite sides either by gripping it at the bow and stern deck plates or, here, on a special whitewater model, by bow and stern thwarts.

comfortable grips here. Carry on opposite sides of the boat for balance and to make it easier to stop and switch every few yards. This method is fine for short carries or for ones with such uneven footing that you are worried about dropping the boat.

Portage Carry

You've arrived at the car. Set the boat down beside the vehicle and about 5 feet away from it. Both of you stand between the car and the boat. Face the boat, each person

Solo portage carry (from left): 1) standing beside the canoe at its midpoint, bend at the knees and grip it by its center thwart. Lift it up onto the shelf of your thighs made by your bent-knee position. 2) Now hoist and with some help from the thighs, bounce the canoe up over your head 3) into the classic portage position. See Chapter 5 for more on portaging.

opposite a bow or stern seat. To avoid back strain, with a straight back, bend at the knees so that the tops of your thighs form slightly angled shelves. Grab the gunwales nearest you and on "three!" lift the boat up so that it rests on the tops of your thighs. From this position, reach across the boat to the other gunwale with one hand while continuing to hold the near side with the other hand, and again on "three!" bounce the canoe up and over your head.

This is called the portage carry because it is the same position you will employ when you want to carry, or portage, the canoe some distance.

(See Chapter 5, page 97, for more information on portaging.) Once the boat is up in this position, it's a simple matter of sliding it onto the roof rack.

TYING THE BOAT DOWN

The thought of a 16-foot canoe coming off your car as you speed along in traffic at 60 miles an hour is nightmarish enough for anyone to take securing the boat seriously. There are many cute systems available. Some employ rubber shock cords that break without warning and send metal clips whizzing past your head (or into it). Others use fancy

straps with buckle ends that hit you on the head when your friend throws them over the car or dent the car roof when they bounce off it.

If you learn a few simple knots, you'll always be able to tie boats down securely with common, dependable rope. Use 1/4-to-3/8-inch-thick nylon or polypropylene rope. Always tie your canoe down in four places: two across the boat secured to the racks, and one at either end secured to the car's tow loops or bumpers. Each cross-tie rope should be twice as long as your rack is

STRETCHING

following stretches are adapted.

LOOSENING UP TO PADDLE Spending a few minutes stretching prior to paddling is a good idea. Many active people disregard stretching, acknowledging its benefits but skipping it to get on with their activity. The choice is yours, but remember that increased flexibility helps you in canoeing and in every other sport you do. If you just can't seem to find the time to stretch, at least go very easy for about 15 minutes when you begin, and go through your whole repertoire of strokes to warm your body up to those motions.

For those wise enough to stretch, here is a group of moves selected with the canoeist in mind. Perform them gently and never pull to the point of inducing pain; stop just as your muscles or tendons begin to resist. The definitive guide to stretching for all sports and activities is *Stretching*, by Bob Anderson, from which the

NECK, BACK, & RIB CAGE Sit on the floor with your

right leg straight. Cross your left foot over your right knee and rest it on the floor. Then rest your right elbow on the outside of your left knee. Now, with your left hand resting on the floor behind you, slowly turn your head to look over your left shoulder. Hold for 15 seconds. Don't hold your breath. Do both sides.

SHOULDERS With arms over head, hold the elbow of one arm with the hand of the other arm and gently pull the elbow behind your wide if you ever plan to tie on more than one boat. End lines should be about 12 feet long.

The more familiar you are with knots, the better you can rig a system of your own, but here is a simple one that has held secure thousands of boats at the nation's largest paddling school without failing. If you need to bone up on your knots, refer to one of the knot handbooks listed in Sources & Resources at the back of this book. CROSS TIES. Loop one end of the rope around the rack, and secure it with a

---

head. Hold for 15 seconds, switch to other side.

NECK & SHOULDER

Lean your head toward your left shoulder as you pull your right arm down and across behind your back with your left hand. Hold an easy stretch for 10 seconds, switch to other side.

CHEST, ARMS, & SHOULDERS

Hold onto a fence, both sides of a doorway, or two sturdy saplings with your arms behind you at shoulder

level. Let your arms straighten as you gently lean forward. Hold your chest up and your chin in.

ARMS, SHOULDERS, & RIBS

With arms extended overhead and palms facing one another, stretch arms upward and slightly back, breathing in as you stretch upward. Hold for 5 to 8 seconds.

SHOULDER & UPPER BACK

To stretch your shoulders and the middle of your upper back, gently pull your elbow across your chest toward your opposite shoulder. Hold for 10 seconds, switch to other side.

✓

GETTING STARTED: CHECKLIST

● Canoe — Essential in most of the situations described below. A perfectly serviceable used aluminum or plastic one can be purchased for as little as $300.

● Paddle — One for each person.

● PFD — Used to be called a life jacket. You want a Coast Guard-approved Type III, which is cut like a vest.

● Clothing — Clothes that you don't mind getting wet: shorts, T-shirt, bathing suit, sneakers.

● Sun Protection — You're going to be out on the water, with reflection to cope with. Take a hat, sunglasses, and sunscreen, If you're sun-sensitive, wear a long-sleeved light-colored cotton shirt. Old white dress shirts are great, adding an air of slouched formality that sits well in this tradition-bound sport.

● Bailer — The best is an old bleach bottle with the bottom cut out. Gallon plastic milk jugs also work well.

figure-8 knot. Pull the other end over the boat. Stand with your shoulder against the boat, and pull down as hard as you can. Take several wraps of rope around the rack to keep the tension twangingly tight. Now tie two half hitches.

END LINES. Many boaters neglect these. End lines hold the boat in place in high crosswinds and prevent you from losing the boat should the rack come unclipped. Always put on end lines. Here's how:

If your canoe has a painter, use it. If not, attach an end line to the boat with a figure-8 knot. Run the rope down from the boat to one of the towing loops under the bumper of your car. Assuming your car has two tow loops, run it through the other and back up to the boat. Pass the rope through the boat's bow loop, and pull down as hard as possible. Finish with a taut-line hitch.

That's it! With your boat now secured against the vicissitudes of wind and freeway traffic, you are safe to proceed to the water.

LOADING AND UNLOADING ALONE

If you have the strength to press 80 pounds above your head, and long enough arms to reach all the way across the center of a canoe, you can simply use a solo version of the technique two paddlers use to pick up a canoe and get it onto your car's roof rack. With a good straight back, lift the boat first to the platform of the tops of your thighs, then reach across to the far gunwale with one hand, and bounce the boat up and over your head. If you are centered on the canoe, this is not as difficult as it sounds.

For those or us who don't easily throw 80 pounds over our heads, there is another method. Roll the boat over so that it is upside down. Pick up one end, and, with your hands above your head, "walk" your hands down the gunwales toward the center of the boat. Before you get to the center, turn around so that you are facing the end you just picked up. Now walk a few steps

ROOF RACKS

The trend among automakers toward increasingly aerodynamic designs has caused consternation among canoeists. Rain gutters, which used to be standard on all car roofs and provided a perfect anchor for roof racks, are going the way of the buggy whip. At one time, all boaters purchased a quartet of tower clamps — called Quik-N-Easys — that fit on all rain gutters. Treated 2-by-4s were bolted to these, and everyone was racked and ready for a cost of about $20.

Now, however, sleek, gutterless cars have spawned at least two companies, Yakima and Thule, that dominate the market with a bewildering variety of racks on which to transport every conceiv-

able outdoor toy. The retailers who carry them will be happy to survey your frictionless bullet of a car and tell you which rack you must buy. Average cost for a basic rack: $135 to $150. And, of course, more for add-ons to hold every new plaything you wish to carry.

You can still get by with foam blocks between the canoe and the roof, along with cross and end tiedowns. However, only the most budget-conscious are going to stay with this system for long. You'll need some racks if you get serious about canoeing.

The anti-technologists among you can still buy Quik-N-Easys for about $45, provided you can find a car with rain gutters. Certain diehard paddlers still frequent the used-car lots looking for these, grumbling, "No gutters, no guts."

Images such as this embody the promise of canoeing: taking up a paddle and setting out on the waters to find adventures both peaceful and exciting from one of the simplest and most graceful craft of all time.

backward to get to the center. Rest the center thwart on your shoulders, and the back end of the boat will rise.

If you don't want to pick up the whole boat, position it upside down beside the car about 6 feet away. Pick up one end, and rest it on the front car rack (the naturally curved ends of the canoe will help keep it from slipping off). Pick up the other end, and gently lift it onto the rear car rack, being careful to keep it from slipping off the front rack. To get the boat off, reverse the process.

To move the boat short distances alone, you can carry it from the side, gripping it by the gunwale. You can, of course, drag the thing to the water, but that is not an option if you have a beautiful wood canoe. It makes a hideous racket if your boat is aluminum, and scratches plastic canoes. Besides, dragging the boat also shows a callous indifference toward the craft on which you will rely for so much. Be kind. Carry your canoe to the water.

> 66 Whatever you can do, or
> dream you can, begin it.
> Boldness has genius, power, and
> magic in it. 99
>
> — Goethe

A T
T H E   W A T E R ' S
E D G E

To learn the first things about canoeing, you need a body of water that gives you at least 200 feet of room to move in any direction, has no current taking you places against your will, and is clean enough that you won't mind swimming in it. Despite the alarming fact that many of our waterways do not meet this last criterion, you should be able to find a piece of water, be it a pond, lake, or lazy river, that fills the bill reasonably near your home. Ideally, your learning spot will have a gradually sloping beach with ample shallows before the water deepens to greater than your body height.

Stick with still water — called flat water by canoeists — at first. If you have aspirations to paddle white water in good control, fine, but do not experiment with moving water until you have real competence in the basic strokes I will explain in Chapter 3. Many canoeists ruefully describe their first canoeing experience as an out-of-control event: putting in on the local creek in flood, careering down the waterway, flipping, and often losing the canoe. Such adventures can make for humorous retelling, but they also can scare people out of the sport and, at worst, end in tragedies that could have been easily avoided. Go to flat water first.

Before you begin paddling for the opposite shore or downriver, take a few moments to stretch your back, shoulder, and arm muscles to prepare them for the task at hand. The above series of simple moves, repeated a few times before you take paddle into your hands, will increase both your performance and pleasure. Twist only as far as is comfortable and do so gently and smoothly; the point is to loosen muscles, not strain them.

You're here. Having unloaded your boat and carried it to the beach or the dock at the water's edge, you and your partner are pumped and ready to leap in and paddle away. Not yet, my friends. Let's get a few basics fixed in our minds and bodies before we go out on the water. The most important concept to learn is *rotation*, which is so central to safe and effective canoe strokes that I don't want you heading out until you feel it and believe in it.

THE IMPORTANCE OF ROTATION

Sit down on the beach or dock. While you're sitting there, hold your hands out in front of you, knuckles up, with arms bent and relaxed. Now loosen up your body a bit by turning at the waist as far as you comfortably can to the right, then to the left. Twist slowly and don't go beyond the comfort zone. Do this several times to feel how far your body lets you twist. Young, supple gymnasts might be able to torque around into a spiral, but the less flexible among us might get only a quarter turn. Regardless of how far you twist, you just proved you can rotate your torso.

Here is the piece of precious information that too many canoeists either never learn or forget when they are under pressure: *Rotation precedes every stroke!*

Why do I make such a big deal of rotation? Because it is central to the Grand Unified Theory of Canoeing and of all other sports: You do things better when you do them in balance, centered over your body. Rotating allows you to generate power without leaning out of balance, side to side. It also lets you use the large muscles of your trunk and back, rather than the

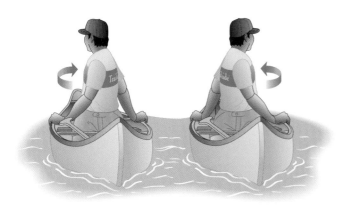

rotate as much as is comfortable for you. With arms bent, try twisting again as far as you can. This is your area of greatest power. Notice how your hands stay in front of your shoulders. Some instructors call this "The Box," asking students to visualize an area in front of their shoulders where they are to keep their hands. Others refer to the area described by the amount of rotation as a "Circle of Power." By any name, rotation is critical to making safe, effective strokes. If you bring your hands back for what you imagine to be greater power, you are courting a strained or dislocated shoulder, as well as putting yourself out of balance.

relatively small, easily strained muscles and joints of your arms and shoulders. Just think of the windup of a discus thrower, the swing of a golfer, even your own frustrated flailing while trying to pull-start your stalled lawn mower — each act uses rotation for maximum power. Furthermore, if you learn to rotate, all the strokes will come more easily and be more effective for you.

If you are confused by the concept of rotating, or twisting forward, try this: Stand facing a wall with your right arm straight out in front of you, hand balled into a fist. Your knuckles should be about 6 inches away from the wall. Now twist forward so that your knuckles touch the wall. You gained that extra 6 inches of reach through rotation alone, and in those 6 inches, the real power of your paddle strokes will be contained. Your body is like a spring winding up to release power.

Notice that I didn't tell you to rotate a specific amount: I said to

INTO THE WATER

"Come, come," you say. "Let's get out on the water and start *paddling!*" I applaud your eagerness, but the time you spend understanding rotation is time well spent.

Now you are hot from all this stretching, and the lake beckons. Fine, let's go out in the canoe. But don't bother bringing paddles. I have a more basic agenda: discovering exactly where your balance point is

how to handle the inevitable, rather than wait for some time when a spill might have more serious consequences. The purpose of these exercises is to combine play with learning. First, put your boat in the water. PUTTING IN FROM A DOCK. Flip the canoe right side up. Stand at its center facing your partner. Grab the boat

Putting In from a Dock. Once the canoe is in the water simply swing it around parallel to the dock, then either hold it in place or tie it to the dock to load it with gear before you gingerly get in. Here a fisherman is about to set out on Cascade Lake in the Adirondack Mountains of New York State.

and learning how to react when you exceed it. In other words, we are going to tip the boat over and cool off.

Yes, yes, I know you want to learn how to paddle, and you don't plan on tipping over. But no one ever does, and you might as well learn right away

with a wide grip at the gunwales on your side while your partner does likewise on the opposite side. Lift it and walk onto the dock. Turn so that the boat is perpendicular to the dock's edge, and tilt it downward and into the water. Once the boat is in the

GEAR TALK

WHICH END IS FORWARD?

To avoid early humiliation, sit in the boat facing the bow. Unsure which is the bow? Look for the thwart or seat that is farther from one end of the boat. That is the bow seat. Sit between it and the bow if you are the bow paddler. Once you have that figured out, the stern seat will be apparent.

The kneeling position is good for posture and maneuverability, but sitting, as above, is preferred by many, and is a welcome change in position on long voyages over open water. With the aid of light-weight nylon camp chairs that provide a measure of back support, sitting can be difficult to resist.

water, simply swing it around parallel to the dock.

FROM A BEACH OR BANK. Carry the boat out into water up to your calves, and set it down.

Getting In

Because the canoe is a narrow craft, many first-timers are worried about capsizing the boat as they get in and before they've even set off. You'll soon believe in the miraculous stability of the craft's design. Until then, get into the boat this way: While a partner steadies the canoe, bending down, grab the gunwales and gently step into the center in front of the thwart or seat from which you will be paddling.

Sitting or Kneeling

Although I have said "sit," remember to assume the kneeling position the moment you get into the canoe — your bottom resting against the thwart or edge of the seat and your knees out as wide as the sides of the boat will allow.

For the purposes of this book, let's assume all strokes are done from a kneeling position. I favor this position because it is the most stable, allows the fullest range of rotation, and is actually the best for your back and spine. There is nothing wrong with sitting on the seat to rest your knees occasionally or even for long spells of straight-ahead paddling, but

Rock the boat gently back and forth by sinking down on one knee, then the other. Keep your arms relaxed, bent at the elbows and with your hands at shoulder height. Resist the urge to grab the gunwales for support. Rock the boat with greater vigor. If you keep your lower body rocking, but your upper body quiet, you'll maintain remarkable stability even as the boat rocks.

for any maneuvers, kneeling is incontestably the best position for a canoeist.

PLAY ON THE WATER

Here we go! You know you are about to get wet (which will feel great), so let's learn something in the process. The exercises that follow (with one exception) can be done either tandem or solo.

Finding Your Balance Point

You are kneeling with your knees out as wide as they can comfortably spread — preferably up against the chine, where the sides of the canoe begin to curve upward from the bottom. *Your* bottom is resting against the thwart or seat behind you. After trying the following balance exercises kneeling, try them sitting up on the seats. You'll see how superior kneeling is.

Rock the boat back and forth gently by sinking down onto one knee and then the other. Keep your arms relaxed, bent at the elbows and with your hands at shoulder height. Don't grab the gunwales for support: You won't find any there. Rock the boat with greater vigor. Notice how it

DID YOU KNOW

The kneeling position in the canoe is one of the best for relief of intraspinal pressure. Tests have shown that of several positions, the worst for building up pressure in the spinal column is sitting with knees drawn up (as in driving, or in "vegging out" in front of the TV); and the best, with the spine straight and supported by the body, were standing with good posture and the canoeist's position. You might have even seen some chairs designed for suffering office workers that replicate the well-supported stance of the canoeist.

Tandem Teamwork. Two whitewater canoeists practice a tandem draw (see Chapter 3, page 54) on the Winooski River in northern Vermont. This move spins their boat on a dime. Note the kneeling positions and good torso rotation of these paddlers.

remains stable as long as your lower body is loose and your upper body stays quiet, with your head staying over your center of gravity? You've just learned another Great Truth of Canoeing: *A canoe is surprisingly stable if you keep your weight centered over your own balance point.*

And where is that? Where the martial artists and dancers have always known it to be: at the stomach, right around the navel. Distrustful of all this Zen talk? OK, but try this. Move your head away from this centered position — say about 6 inches over the outside edge of the canoe. Boat got awfully tippy, didn't it? Sure it did, just as your body got rigid and top-heavy. All the strokes you're about to learn are less important than this

central issue of balance. Balance is what will allow you to take confident strokes from a secure platform when the boat is in turbulent waters.

"But," you ask, "how can I get my paddle in the water if I am supposed to keep this centered position?"

Recall our rotation mantra. You can always get a good clean reach to the water while staying in balance if you rotate before the stroke. Try it. Imagine you have a paddle in your hands. Twist as far as is comfortable toward your paddling side (choose whichever side feels natural). Notice how easy it is to get your hands out over the water? Now try it to the other side. If you are learning with a partner, try twisting as far as possible to opposite sides.

Tandem Trust Excersise

This move may look outlandish, but it's a superb way to gain trust in your paddling partner and in the ability of your canoe to remain upright. It's also a pretty good lead-up to getting wet and to losing your hat.

If you are fairly flexible, you should be able to reach across the canoe with your right hand in front of you and grab the left gunwale of the boat. Look back over your left shoulder toward the stern. If you can, try twisting far enough to grab the far gunwale with your left hand. That's rotation! Try doing it the opposite way. It makes an excellent stretching exercise as well. Notice how the boat is not one whit less steady. That's the secret: Full power is available to you from a stable boat.

Stability Games

SOLO. Let's learn where the boat becomes unstable and, in the process, find out what to do when we tip the thing over, as all canoeists inevitably do. If you're alone, keep your hands out to your sides and rock the boat with more and more force. If you're practicing what I preach, you'll find that the boat is difficult to flip. Be daring. Move your head farther and farther from the center of the boat. You'll go over.

TANDEM. If in tandem, try this entertaining game. Sit astride your respective thwarts or seats facing each other and the centerline of the boat. Grabbing the gunwales — or the seat itself — try leaning out as far as possible. You'll find two things: First, it is possible to adjust for each other's leans enough to really hang over the side of the boat — even to get your heads wet; and second, by communicating, you can actually sit back up.

If all else fails, and your balance is so perfect that you cannot flip the boat, grab one of the gunwales and pull or push on it for support. That is what most novice canoeists do when they have begun to lose their balance, and it works every time for flipping the boat. You are either pushing it out from under you or pulling it up over you. In either case, the result is swift and dramatic.

WHEN YOU GO IN THE DRINK
Re-Entering a Swamped Canoe

Welcome to the club! You are now a

Like the ski instructor who insists on his students falling in order to rid them of some of their fear of falling, we strongly believe in purposefully capsizing canoes. There is no other way to prepare for the inevitable moment when you accidentally flip. Besides, it's good fun.

member of one of the two inclusive groups in canoeing: those who have flipped, and those who will. Here's what to do when you have. First, try getting back into the swamped boat. This will lay the groundwork for the more athletic maneuver of getting back into a dry one.

You must attempt to get back in over the gunwales near the ends of the boat, where it is easier to reach across than it is at the widest point amidships. If you try to pull yourself in at the middle, it's difficult to reach the far gunwale for balance and you're likely to pull the boat over onto yourself. Practice the smooth motion of reaching across the boat and sliding yourself up and into it, bottom first. If you have a partner, he can steady the boat from the other

side as you do this. If not, you must move more gently.

Re-Entering an Upright Canoe

As you find new and interesting ways to fall out of your canoe, you'll eventually surprise yourself with the "dry exit." Much to the delight of your companions in nearby boats, this maneuver will involve your leaving the boat without flipping it. Typically, it happens in a moment of inattention, when you catch the paddle against the side of the canoe and sort of "trip" over it, levering yourself out. There are many antic variations, but be assured that it does happen and that the time will come when you find yourself in deep water with your boat upright and dry beside you. You will then be glad that you practiced your

Re-entering a Swamped Boat

1) Grab the gunwale by reaching over the bottom of the hull and pull it toward you to right the boat. 2) Get back in over the gunwales at either end of the boat. 3) When your hips are over the gunwale, twist your body so you can drag your legs into the boat. This move is seldom graceful, but always amusing, at least to onlookers.

Re-entering an Upright Boat

Re-entering a swamped canoe is merely a preparation for the more difficult maneuver of getting back into an upright one. It is essentially the same move — 1) grasp the gunwales with both hands; 2) using legs to kick yourself up out of the water and arms to lever yourself, hoist your torso over the boat; and 3) flip over. It is easier said (and illustrated) than done.

re-entry drills when the boat was swamped. Getting back into a dry boat requires more oomph but works on the same principle.

Swim to the end of the boat. If you still have your paddle, stow it in the boat. Now, from the water, grab the gunwale closest to you with one hand, and reach across the boat to the other gunwale with your free hand. Have your partner, if he is also out, stabilize the boat from the other side by leaning slightly away from the side over which you are getting in. It's nearly impossible to get back in elegantly: Most canoeists haul themselves aboard stomach first with all the elegance of an elephant seal galumphing over dry land, then roll over to settle their bottom onto the bottom of the canoe. When you end up in the boat, you will tend to be facing toward the side you galumphed in on. If your partner gets in at the same time as you from the opposite side, you'll appear reasonably coordinated. Usually, hilarity seizes one or both people at about this point, resulting in loud splashes and gales of choked laughter. Practice this when it is funny, so it will work for you when the situation is not.

Getting back into an upright canoe alone is even more difficult. Your companions in other boats may, after they have enjoyed your futile attempts, steady your boat to make the job easier.

Emptying a Canoe in Deep Water

When faced with a swamped canoe, what next? How to bail it out? Surprisingly, you have several options. It is possible to get back in and rock the boat clear of much of its water, though this takes more practice and patience than most sane people possess. It is easier to start with a boat equipped with sufficient flotation to keep the gunwales above the waterline even when fully swamped. Then,

SAFETY IN NUMBERS

Most Coast Guard accident reports read along the same lines: Solitary person in a boat — no PFD. Just as the PFD adds a huge measure of safety to messing about in boats, so does paddling with partners. The preferred group size is three boats. This provides pleasure in company, the ability to learn a good deal by analyzing each other's strokes, and a comforting margin of safety if one boat swamps or there is a medical emergency (see Chapter 9, "Whitewater Features and Safety," for further discussion).

But there are special pleasures to be had in solitary lake canoeing, and I would no more suggest prohibitions on it than I would try to talk people out of going for a walk by themselves. If you want to paddle alone, exercise a few commonsense precautions: Let someone know where you are going and when you expect to return, take your PFD with you, and stay reasonably close to shore. "Reasonably close" means the distance you are able to swim on your own, and considerations such as water and air temperature, currents, waves, and wind must be factored into that distance. Paddling white water alone is never a good idea: Too many variables exist beyond your control.

Rocking the Boat Dry

1) Swim to one end or the other and press down. Then abruptly and vigorously push away from you. This flushes some of the water out. 2) Now swim to the middle of the side of the boat, push down on the near gunwale until it is under water and, again, abruptly and vigorously push away. With practice, these two moves will flush the boat of most of its water.

floating beside it, you can bail the boat out enough to allow you to get in and finish the job.

Another option is to push down on one end of the canoe, then abruptly, vigorously push it away from you, causing some of the water to be flushed out. Next, swim to the side of the boat, push down on the near gunwale so that it is underwater, and again, push the boat forcefully away from you. Done correctly, this pushes the boat out from under the water; it rights itself with only a fraction of the original water remaining inside.

The easiest deep-water rescue is the gunwale-over-gunwale method. This requires another boat, but canoeing is safest in groups of at least three boats anyway. Make a T with the end of the swamped boat up against the midships of a fully floating canoe. The canoeist in the water then flips the swamped boat

upside down and pushes down on the end farthest from the rescue boat. The opposite end of the swamped canoe — the one against the rescue boat — rises, allowing the dry paddler to lift it over his boat. He then slides the swamped canoe up until it is centered over the rescue boat. Now the formerly swamped canoe is rolled upright and slid back into the water. This procedure is very stable and can be done quickly with practice.

Emptying a Canoe in Shallow Water

Whenever you're emptying a canoe, try to pick up only the boat, not the heavy water in it. That means you want to flip the boat upside down first. TANDEM. Stand beside the ends of the boat, flip it over, lift it straight up, then twist it over so that it is right side up.

SOLO. If the water is waist-deep, it's easiest to get under the canoe so that

Gunwale-Over-Gunwale Rescue

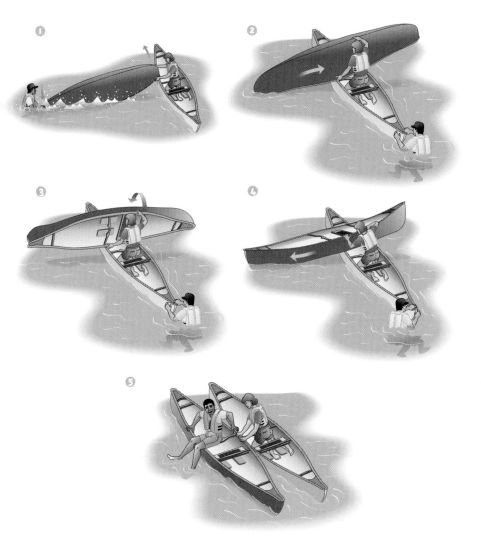

The classic method of emptying a canoe in parties of two or more boats, in this instance two solo boats. 1) Position the capsized boat so that it is perpendicular to the upright one. Now the swimmer presses down on one end of the capsized boat to bring the opposite end out of the water and up over the gunwale of the upright boat. 2) From there the dry paddler can pull the canoe up and over both of her gunwales, an action that drains it of most of its water. 3) Now (and this is when light-weight models count for something) she flips the boat upright as the swimmer steadies her boat from one end. 4) Next, she slides the upright boat back into the water. 5) With the two boats side-by-side, the dry canoeist grips the gunwales of the two to steady them as the swimmer re-enters his canoe. In cold deep water far from shore, this method can save lives. Practice it under less threatening conditions.

End of a day of paddling on the Missinaibi River in Ontario, Canada. Note the spare paddles lashed to the gunwales. And lest you assume that all books picture ideal settings, note that these canoeists are wearing beekeeper's hats in an effort to keep the notorious Canadian black flies at bay.

the center thwart or seat is on your shoulders. Now stand up, and tip and toss the boat upright away from you.

If that sounds like too much lifting, you can simply get the canoe resting upside down on the shore, then turn it over. Remember, the idea is to lift the boat only, not the extra tonnage of water.

◼

You've covered a lot of ground — I mean water. You can load the boat on your car and get it into and out of the water. You understand how to stay balanced and know what to do if the thing tips over. It's time, at last, to learn what to do with the elegant wand called the paddle.

B A S I C
T A N D E M
S T R O K E S

I f you possibly can, learn to canoe with a partner. Tandem strokes will teach you how to move the ends of the boat around its central pivot point, it is great to have the company, and ideally, you want another person to become addicted to this sport so that you'll be able to share camping adventures on lakes or run rivers together when you eventually get out on moving water. So start with a partner. There is nothing finer than the shared excitement of learning a new sport together, particularly one where your individual efforts are designed to complement and support another person's efforts. If, however, a partner is not available or going it alone is your preference, skip to Chapter 4: "Solo and Cross-Bow Strokes."

HOLDING THE PADDLE
Grip and Shaft Hands

For clarity and simplicity, I will describe all strokes in this chapter from the point of view of a right-handed stern paddler, meaning that the stern paddler's "on-side" is to the right side of the boat. This then dictates that the bow paddler's on-side is to the left side of the boat.

Kneeling in your by now comfortably balanced stance in the stern of the canoe, grab the paddle by its T

Indicator Thumb

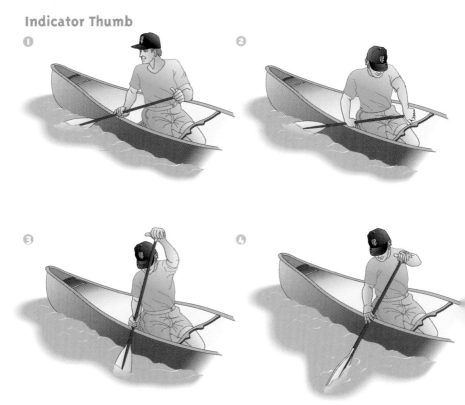

Stick the thumb of your grip hand out to quickly and easily remind yourself of how to correctly hold the paddle for various strokes. The most common position is for the forward stroke, when the indicator thumb sticks straight out, perpendicular to the side of the boat. Here are some trickier positions: 1) Thumb Up. This is the position of the blade at the end of a pry stroke (see page 62). 2) Thumb Down. Here is the correct position for the end of the J stroke (see page 63). Note that the shaft-hand wrist is bent down also, following the grip-hand wrist. 3) Thumb Back. This is the position of the grip hand as the paddle nears the end of a draw. At this point you may either drop the grip hand forward to slice the paddle out of the water or 4) turn the grip thumb outward for a feathering recovery in preparation for a second draw stroke.

grip with your left hand. Simply make a fist around the grip, and you are holding it correctly. With your right hand, grab the paddle around the shaft 8 to 12 inches above the blade. You'll find that you move your lower, or shaft, hand around on the paddle a fair amount, depending on the needs of the stroke, but your top, or grip, hand will always hold the paddle the same way. Throughout this book, I will refer to the hand at the top of the paddle as the *grip hand*, and the hand that holds the shaft above the paddle's blade as the *shaft hand*.

Indicator Thumb

Here's a device for helping you to learn how to hold the paddle correctly for the various strokes. Put the paddle in the water beside the canoe with its blade perpendicular to the side of the boat as if you were about to take a forward stroke. Stick your grip-hand thumb out. Notice how it points out straight sideways? Now try sliding the blade around in the water, directing it with the thumb of your grip hand. If your thumb is sticking out sideways, the paddle slices out of the water away from the boat. If you twist your wrist so that your grip-hand thumb points back, the paddle blade is parallel to the boat and slices back. If you point forward with your thumb, it feels natural to slice the blade out forward.

Let's call the grip-hand thumb that directs the paddle the *indicator thumb*. This is a useful device to help you gain dexterity with the paddle, and I will refer to your indicator thumb in teaching you new strokes. In actual paddling, you'll simply make a fist around the grip, but when I am teaching a stroke, I may ask you to be conscious of the direction in which your indicator thumb would be pointing if it were extended.

The Power Face
Now let's look at the paddle. Pretend you are about to take a forward stroke on the right side of the canoe. The face of the paddle blade that you are pulling through the water toward you is the *power face*: the opposite side, the *non-power face*. While you are learning strokes, it's a good idea always to use the same power face for

consistency. If your paddle has a logo on one side, make that side the power face. Otherwise, write your name on the power face.

SWEEP STROKES
Before you can do anything in a canoe — even before you go forward — you must be able to turn it in a circle. Many beginners do just fine by switching their paddle side to side and paddling forward or backward, slowing one side and then the other so that the boat turns like an oil tanker. Not a pretty picture. You want precise control, and that can quickly be yours with the sweep and draw strokes. They are remarkably effective and simple, provided you use the mantra of rotation you learned in Chapter 2 and take your time to do each one right. Remember, too, that tandem paddlers always paddle on opposite sides of the boat.

Sweeps are wide strokes meant to turn the boat while maintaining forward momentum. You want to keep your hands low — somewhere between your shoulders and waist — and think of the paddle blade following a wide arc between you and the end of the canoe to which you are closest. The pivot point of the boat is in the middle. As tandem paddlers, you want to turn the ends. To do so, keep your strokes between your position in the canoe and the end of the boat nearest you.

Because the sweeps have dif-

THE BOW PADDLER IS IN CHARGE

One of the few difficulties of tandem canoeing among beginners is agreeing on who is in charge, the bow paddler or the stern paddler. There should be no debate: The bow paddler makes turning decisions, and the stern paddler follows and complements those decisions, period.

Why are there are so many squabbles, particularly among male and female tandem teams? Because even people who know little about canoeing are dimly aware that the steering strokes are taken from the stern. They expand on this and conclude that the stern paddler makes all the calls regarding direction. That isn't so, but the average American male seems to think that canoeing ability is his by birthright, takes the stern, does all the wrong strokes, and bellows conflicting commands at his hapless wife (or girlfriend) in the bow. Small wonder that tandem canoeing is thought of as the burial ground of relationships. It doesn't have to be.

It is true that maintaining a course over distance is the job of the stern paddler, who has primary responsibility for correction strokes (see page 61). But sudden, precise changes in direction must be made from the bow, often because the bow paddler can see an obstacle to be avoided long before the stern paddler can. In cases such as this, there is no time to question the bow's call: The stern must follow. That way, even if a mistake is made and the obstacle is bumped, you are acting as a team, rather than two people struggling against each other. Every bow stroke has a stern stroke that complements it so that both paddlers are working toward the same end, whether that be to make a wide or a sharp right or left turn, to slow the canoe, stop it, reverse directions, or even to pull it directly sideways with draw strokes. If the stern paddler is opposing the bow paddler's moves, the boat will likely not change course at all, sometimes with unpleasant consequences.

To cement this idea of complementary strokes, *every* tandem team should spend at least a little while exchanging positions to understand the needs of the opposite end of the boat. Once you've done this, the habitual bow paddler will try to give the stern more time to follow strokes, and the habitual stern paddler will learn what the river looks like from the bow of a canoe — and how suddenly obstructions can appear.

Bow Forward Sweep

Bow Reverse Sweep

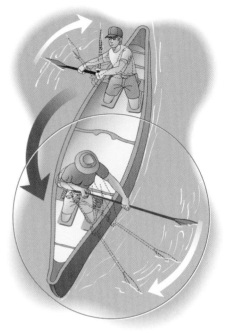

This stroke turns the boat toward the bow pad-dler's off- (or opposite) side yet also maintains forward momentum. Note the bent elbow and low hand position of the grip-hand (right) arm, and the forward extension of the shaft-hand (left) arm. In tandem situations, combining it with a stern reverse sweep turns the boat more abruptly.

This stroke turns the boat toward the paddler's on- (or same) side. Note the torso rotation toward the on-side, and the way the grip hand holds the end of the paddle low and near the center of the paddler, acting as a fulcrum from which the shaft hand levers the paddle forward. Also note that the paddle enters the water at the boater's hips, *not* behind them. Again, in tandem situations, the opposing stroke, a stern forward sweep, turns the canoe that much faster.

ferent effects when done by bow and stern paddlers, I will explain them for each position, then describe how to use them to complement each other.

Bow Sweeps

BOW FORWARD SWEEP. In the bow, twist as far forward as is comfortable and bury the blade in the water. Your grip-hand arm is bent and close to

you, and your shaft-hand arm is extended well forward but not rigidly locked. Remember, your hands are low. Your grip-hand indicator thumb should be sticking straight up.

Do the stroke by pushing out — away from the boat — with both hands: the natural unwinding of the body from its rotated position will bring the paddle out in an arc. See

Like the bow forward sweep, the stern forward sweep turns the boat to the paddler's off-side yet maintains some forward momentum. Since the bow paddler takes the lead, this stroke is one possible response to a bow reverse sweep if a fairly quick turn is needed. Note that the paddle enters the water just forward of the paddler's waist.

Stern Forward Sweep

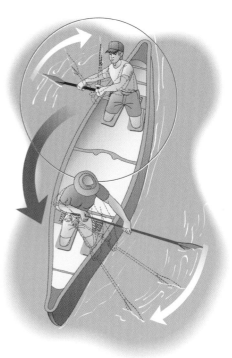

how the stroke pushes the bow away toward your opposite side? Now pick the paddle up when it is about equal with your body. No going behind you toward the middle of the canoe; the strongest phase of the forward sweep is the initial one, where the paddle is fully loaded and pushing the bow around.

BOW REVERSE SWEEP. This has limited use for the bow paddler but should be learned nevertheless. Simply do a mirror image of the forward sweep. Start with low hands out to the side, and push the non-power face out in an arc toward the bow. You should end in the position from which you began your forward sweep. This stroke has impressive turning power,

P R A C T I C E   D R I L L

TANDEM SWEEPS

Let the bow person initiate a turn by starting to do a forward sweep. The stern person should then help out with the complementary stroke, the reverse sweep. Once the boat is turning well, switch paddling sides and keep the boat moving in the same direction without stopping the turn. Keep some momentum up. After a few turns, and without switching sides, stop your turn and, again with sweep strokes only, get the boat turning in the opposite direction. If you can consistently do this as a team, using sweeps to turn the boat in either direction from either paddling side, you know your sweeps.

This stroke complements the bow paddler's forward sweep when quite rapid turning is required. For a more gradual turn, the stern paddler could continue making forward strokes as the bow paddler executed a few forward sweeps. Note that the stern paddler removes his blade just forward of his hips; moving it any farther forward wastes energy.

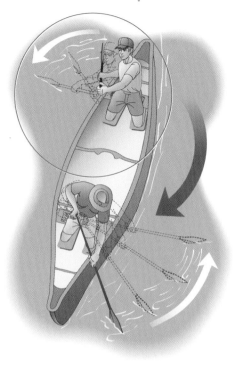

but because it slows the boat down, its usefulness is limited.

Using just the forward sweep stroke, the bow paddler should be able to turn the boat in a complete circle alone. Try just that. Now try going the opposite way, using the reverse sweep stroke. Note that the boat is turning around in close to its own length. However, it's time for some help. Let's get the stern partner in the picture.

Stern Sweeps

You've been watching your partner in the bow crank the boat around. How

---

TECHNIQUE TIP

FEATHERING

Feathering, also called in-water recovery, is the ability to slide the paddle blade around in the water without moving the boat. It involves slicing the blade through the water's edge first rather than power face first. When you become proficient at feathering, you can slice the paddle back out to the point where your stroke began and either take it out of the water or take another stroke if one is needed. Practice feathering on all your strokes: It will give them fluency and grace.

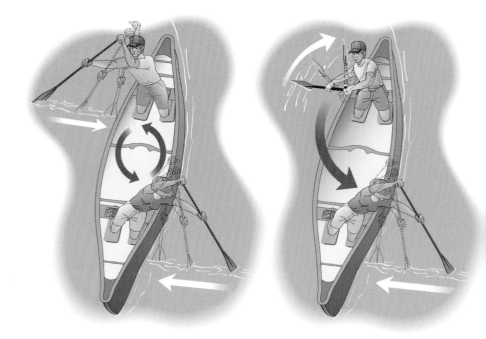

Properly executed, this combination of strokes spins a canoe on a dime. The draw stroke pulls the boat toward the paddle blade, which is planted into the water directly off the paddler's on-side. Note the rotation of the bow paddler's torso as she plants the blade. Also look at the position of the blade — *perpendicular* to the boat's side — as the stroke ends. Feathering the paddle in this way allows the blade to be sliced either out of the water for a change of stroke, or back through the water for a second draw.

This tandem combination produces a strong, sharp turn without eliminating all forward momentum. It can be up to the stern paddler to decide how to respond to the strokes the bow paddler initiates, depending on what's ahead. Both paddlers must be aware of what is down-stream, but only time spent paddling together provides the experience that yields smoothly coordinated tandem strokes.

do you help? *By doing the opposite stroke at the same time.* If your bow paddler is turning the boat toward her side with reverse sweeps, you can keep the boat turning in the same direction by pulling the stern around using forward sweeps.

STERN FORWARD SWEEP. With your hands low, indicator thumb pointing up, begin the forward sweep out at your side and take it back toward the stern. Don't reach forward to the center of the canoe to start the stroke; that's counterproductive, because you want to turn your end of the canoe. Follow your paddle blade around toward the stern with your eyes to help you properly rotate your body.

STERN REVERSE SWEEP. Keeping your hands low, your indicator thumb up, rotate as far toward the stern as you can. Bury the blade in the water as close to the stern as possible, and push the non-power face out in a wide arc until it is equal with your knees, then simply lift the paddle out. This is one of the strongest strokes in canoeing — the leverage produced is enormous, particularly at the "catch," or first phase of the stroke. Try doing it at the same time your partner is doing a forward sweep, and watch how the boat turns on a dime.

DRAW STROKES

You can turn the boat smoothly, but what about side-to-side control? Did you know that you can even move a canoe dead sideways? That's what draw strokes are for. Once you have learned them, you'll know more than two-thirds of the canoeing strokes there are. With draws, you can spin the boat, move it sideways, or any small variant in between. Let's look at the bow paddler's moves first, then see how the stern paddler can complement her stroke.

Bow Draw

Rotate toward your paddling side first. Then turn so that your chest is facing that side. Now, reach out over the water with both hands. Your paddle should be vertical as you face it — your grip hand straight over your shaft hand — and you should be looking at the power face of the blade. Your grip hand's indicator thumb should point

---

T E C H N I Q U E   T I P

PULL THROUGH THE TURN

All too often, bow paddlers make a decisive and sudden move around an obstruction, then turn to watch it to see if the boat will clear. Don't look back! Bow paddlers need to remember to pull the boat past the obstruction they have just avoided.

The bow person has to move only a few feet of canoe to get around something. The stern person has all the rest of the boat and needs help. Having made the stroke to initiate a sudden turn, the bow paddler should make several powerful forward strokes. This will keep the boat moving forward past the obstruction, allowing the stern paddler first to take the complementary stroke to help turn the boat, then to hold the stern off the obstruction with either draws or pries. Think of pulling the middle of the boat past the obstruction before you turn to look, if look you must. Even when you are starting out on a lake and practicing maneuvers around fixed obstructions, follow this rule.

The Pushaway

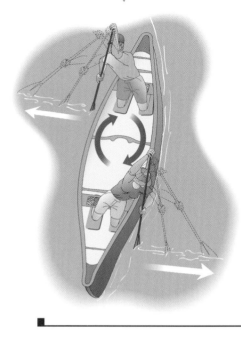

back toward the stern of the canoe.

Push *down* with your grip hand. This will load the blade and bring the boat toward the paddle.

Before the paddle hits the side of the boat, which it will do before you know it, drop your grip hand forward, pivoting the paddle and bringing the blade up out of the water. At the end of the stroke, your indicator thumb should point straight up.

Stern Draw

First, try doing this exactly as your bow partner does it, but on *your* on-

PUSHING DOWN AT THE FORWARD STROKE "CATCH"

Some things I suggest might seem to go against what feels natural, and nothing more so than when I tell you *not* to pull back with the shaft hand on the forward stroke. "Why not?" you ask, "Don't you need to pull yourself through the water with the paddle?"

Well, you are certainly using the paddle to move the boat, but not in the way that you think. The well-placed, fully loaded paddle actually stays in about the same place, while

the boat moves up to and past it. If you simply yank on the paddle with your shaft hand, you are moving it behind you as the boat goes forward, not only wasting energy but slowing the boat down.

By stressing the forward twist of body rotation, you are pushing the paddle straight down into the water, burying the blade, and getting the best load on the paddle. "But," you insist, "why doesn't the paddle just dive straight down with no resistance?"

Because of the way your body has rotated. You are loading the paddle vertically up in front of you.

side, opposite hers. Time your stroke so that your paddle enters the water at the same time as your partner's. The boat will spin easily toward your bow partner's side — the left, since you are paddling on the right side.

After practicing that a few times, do the stroke more like your forward sweep: lower your hands, and try to emphasize pulling the power face of the paddle toward the stern. This low-handed version of the draw is the one that stern paddlers most often employ, as you will learn when you begin to make your way down white water. There will also be times when the bow paddler executes a pure draw to pull the bow away from an oncoming rock or scary wave. Then, the best complementary stroke for the stern paddler to take could be the stern draw, which helps turn the boat *and* maintain forward momentum, which is vital to keeping control on white water. So remember this: high hands on the draw if you simply want to spin the boat; low hands (more like a forward sweep) when you want to turn the boat and keep it moving ahead.

The Pushaway

The exact reverse of the standard draw is a long-ignored, old-fashioned stroke called the pushaway. To do it, begin as if you had just finished a

---

As your body unwinds from that full twist forward (remember the way you got your extra twist with your fist toward the wall in Chapter 2?), you are pulling the boat with your body up to and past the fixed paddle. Freeze-frame shots of Olympic canoeists in full sprints show that the paddle *always* stays fixed in the water, while the boat moves past. The emphasis on rotating forward and loading downward allows the catch to take place in front of the paddler, where it should. By the time the paddle is back equal with the canoeist's hips, it should be either coming out of the water or be in place for a corrective steering stroke.

"But," you contend, "I can feel the resistance of the paddle as I pull on it!"

Sorry. What you have felt is simply water being lifted by the blade as the paddle comes past you. In other words, you are picking up pounds of water on every stroke. Getting an extra workout, perhaps, but not improving the forward speed of the canoe. Trust me on this one: Once you've learned this principle, your boat will move more quickly with less effort.

Forward Stroke

Back Stroke

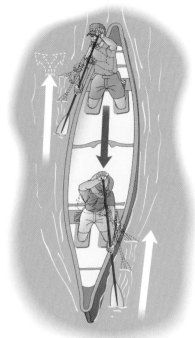

Remember three things for this fundamental stroke: 1) Wind up your rotation as if you were going to do a forward sweep; 2) then push down with your grip hand to bury the blade in the water; 3) and lift the paddle out of the water when it comes alongside your hips.

1) Wind up your torso so that you are looking back over your on-side shoulder. 2) With paddle vertical, push down with your shaft hand to bury the blade in the water. 3) Push the non-power face of the blade forward just past your knees. 4) Pick up your shaft hand to remove blade from water.

draw: facing your paddling side with the paddle parallel to the gunwales, indicator thumb up.

Drop the paddle into the water, slicing the blade forward until the paddle is vertical, with the grip hand over the shaft hand.

Push straight out with both hands. The boat will move away from the paddle.

When you have pushed out to the extent of your balance, drop your

grip hand forward just as you do at the end of a draw while picking up your shaft hand to clear the blade from the water.

Why teach the pushaway at all? You won't use it much, but it is excellent for two things: learning precise side-to-side control, and forcing you to utilize rotation on all your strokes. It is best thought of as a stepping-stone to mastering other strokes, but also teaches the paddle dexterity that makes canoeing so rewarding.

FORWARD STROKE

The forward stroke is one of the most exhaustively analyzed and debated moves in canoeing. Instructors and Olympic flatwater coaches have heated arguments over its finer points. I'm going to give it more space later, but I give it relatively short shrift when teaching the starter strokes. Let's keep it simple: All I want you to do for a forward stroke are three things:

1. Wind up the rotation as if you were going to do a forward sweep, *but keep the paddle as vertical as possible*, not low.

2. When you've wound up as far as possible, *push down* with the grip hand and arm to bury the paddle in the water. Remember, *down* with the grip hand. Don't pull back with the shaft hand as many people do.

3. Lift the paddle out of the water when it comes alongside your hips. You've used up your rotation: Get the paddle out of the water for another windup and stroke by lifting your shaft

---

FEELING THE MOMENT OF CATCH

Okay, Ace, you charged out on the water, the boat looped around out of control, and you're back at the dock to try to understand things a little better. Let's feel all that rotational power and learn the strokes while we are sitting beside the water, best of all on a dock or at the side of a pool. If these aren't available, you can practice standing knee-deep in water. This isn't just silly: When you are stationary, you can feel the full power generated by a stroke at the precise point in the water where the resistance is greatest. In a canoe, the boat will move before

you fully feel that point.

FORWARD STROKE: Twist as far forward as is comfortable, and concentrate on pushing *down* with the grip hand at the moment of "loading," or "catch," of the paddle. You only need to push the paddle in far enough to cover the blade. Feel the power? Next time, when your paddle enters the water, try pulling back with the lower hand, as most novice paddlers do. Notice the relative lack of resistance?

DRAW AND RECOVERY: Turn and face your paddling side *before* you put the paddle in the water. Then pull the paddle toward you, making sure the top

continued on page 60

FEELING THE MOMENT
continued from page 59

hand is out over the water, *not* near your throat or head. Just before the paddle hits the dock, turn your indicator thumb to point away from you (during the draw it points back). See how that turns the paddle blade perpendicular to the side of the dock? Now slice the paddle back out to the beginning of the draw. Do this until you can take five repeated draws without taking the paddle out of the water. You've just learned to *feather* your paddle.

FORWARD SWEEP: Rotate forward as far as is comfortable. Keep your hands at chest level. When you begin your sweep, emphasize pushing *out* with both hands. Straight out, not pulling back. This is an important distinction: When you do it right, you will feel the same kind of catch as you do on a downward-loaded forward stroke.

REVERSE SWEEP: This time rotate as far back as is comfortable. Place the paddle in the water, and emphasize pushing *out*, not forward, with the grip hand. Feel the resistance in your lower arm and stomach.

hand straight out to the side and lowering your grip hand across your chest.

That's it. At this point, all I want you to feel is the moment of catch, or "loading" of the paddle, when you push down on the grip hand. You will feel the boat jump forward and feel as if the paddle were set in something solid. It is.

BACK STROKE

Wind up your torso so that you are looking back over your paddling-side shoulder toward the stern, as for a reverse sweep, but in this case, the paddle is vertical, and your grip-hand indicator thumb is pointing out, away from the boat. Your grip hand should be about head level.

Push down with your shaft hand to bury the blade in the water. You will be pushing the non-power face of the paddle forward through the water. Once the paddle has passed your knees, pick up the shaft hand to take the blade out of the water.

Practice this as a team: When you both do the same stroke, the boat will move forward or backward. When the stern person does the opposite stroke from the bow paddler (for example, a forward stroke while the bow person executes a back stroke), the boat will turn, though not as smoothly as it does with sweeps.

The Pry Stroke

One of two correction strokes that only the stern paddler makes, the pry keeps your canoe heading straight. On a forward stroke, keep rotating your torso *beyond* the point at your hips where you'd normally remove the paddle. 1) As the paddle passes your hips, rest your shaft hand on the gunwale while still holding onto the shaft. With the indicator thumb of your grip hand *up*, push the grip hand out over the water, keeping your shaft hand on the gunwale. 2) To make the correction, *pull* your grip hand back across your chest, maintaining a hold on the gunwale with your shaft hand.

Try both these maneuvers.

■

You and your partner have learned a lot in a short time. It is time to take a break for lunch and contemplate your recent successes. Before you go, however, try paddling off toward an object several hundred yards away. Try to keep the boat heading straight. After all, you know the turning strokes. All you should have to do is paddle together with equal force on forward strokes, and the boat should go reasonably straight, perhaps corrected with the occasional draw or sweep. Try it.

By the time you've returned to your starting point, you'll have noticed that the canoe wants to turn. All the time. It has a mind of its own and apparently has no intention of going straight. You were able to regulate its behavior somewhat with great effort and some application of the strokes you have learned, but you are worn out. What's the solution? Relax, pull the canoe up on shore, and enjoy lunch. We're going to talk about the technique that will tame that wild horse lying next to you.

CORRECTION STROKES

You may have seen pictures of a lone canoeist leaving a beautifully straight wake across a lake at sunrise. That guy doesn't switch sides, you think. How does he keep going straight? The answer is simple, if subtle: At the end of almost every forward stroke, the experienced canoeist makes a small correction to adjust the boat's tendency to turn away from the side where power is applied. So what will you do? You will learn the

The other stern correction stroke is more efficient and best employed once you've gotten up
to speed. 1) As the paddle passes your hips, turn
your indicator thumb *down* so that the knuckles
of both hands face the water. 2) To make the
correction, push the bent wrist of your shaft
hand away from the boat without touching the
gunwale.

The J-Stroke

correction strokes: the stern pry for
big corrections, and the J stroke for
smaller ones. A good way to distin-
guish between the two is to think of
starting from a dead stop. First you
will need the pry to check the boat's
strong tendency to turn away from
you during the initial powerful forward strokes that get the boat under
way. Then the J stroke will come into
play for smaller corrections as you
get up to and maintain speed.

Only the stern paddler (or the
solo paddler) does the correction
strokes. The bow paddler provides
pure forward force without correction.

The Pry

Here's how to keep in check the
canoe's tendency to turn away from
your paddling side.

As you finish the powerful catch
phase of your forward stroke, your
body is rotating toward your paddling side. Fine, keep turning.

As the paddle passes your hips,
rest your shaft hand on the gunwale
of the boat while still holding onto
the paddle. Turn the indicator thumb
of your grip hand *up*. Now rotate as
far as you comfortably can, and take
care to push the grip hand *out* over
the water, keeping your shaft hand
on the gunwale.

66 Look here!" (said the water
rat), "If you've really nothing else
on hand this morning, supposing
we drop down the river together,
and have a long day of it?" The
mole waggled his toes from sheer
happiness, spread his chest with a
sigh of full contentment, and
leaned back blissfully... "What a
day I'm having!" he said. "Let us
start at once! 99

— Kenneth Graham,
The Wind in the Willows

To make the correction, pull *only* your grip hand back across your chest. Your shaft hand continues to hold the paddle on the gunwale. You are using the gunwale as a fulcrum off of which to lever the paddle. Don't pull your grip hand any farther across the boat than the center of your chest, or your paddle will lever out so far that you'll kill much of the boat's initial speed.

After about three or four strokes ending with pries, you'll have picked up some momentum. There is no longer any need for the powerful lever of the pry on every correction stroke. In fact, it's not a good idea to use the pry for more than a few initial start-up strokes, because the pry, no matter how well done, creates more drag and slows the boat more than the J. Here's how to do the signature correction stroke of classic canoeing.

The J Stroke

Take the same kind of forward stroke as you always do: one with good rotation, arm extension, and a positive downward catch.

As the paddle begins to pass your hips, turn your indicator thumb *down* by twisting your wrist down, or clockwise, so that your knuckles face the water. Your shaft hand will also bend down at the wrist. The knuckles of both hands should be turned down. You can push the bent wrist of your shaft hand away from the boat without touching the gunwale, or you can rest the shaft on the gunwale and pull your grip hand across your chest as you did with the pry. The first method is the more traditional J stroke born of wooden boats and lake canoeing, while the second is the modern J stroke that takes advantage of more durable boat materials. In

PRACTICE DRILL

COMBINING STROKES

To practice a combination of the strokes you have learned, paddle toward a stationary object: a dock, a moored boat, or the shore. Go slowly. Try "parallel parking" your canoe with the gentlest of touches against the object using only your paddles in the water to prevent bumping it. Using draw strokes, turn your canoe parallel to the object. Stop your boat with forward and back strokes. Now move the boat dead sideways to dock it. This will involve one partner doing draws and the other doing pushaways. Be sure that you apply equal pressure to make the boat to go sideways. Generally the drawing side overpowers the pushaway side. Once you have gently touched the dock, draw straight away from it, turn, and paddle away.

either version, the paddle comes away from the boat and out of the water quickly.

Pry or J Stroke?

Use each stroke for what it does best. The pry has more leverage: Use it to make big adjustments in angle and when your boat is getting up to speed. The J is smoother and more integrated with your forward stroke: Use it to keep yourself on line when you're happy with your general direction.

Once you have figured out the mechanics of the correction strokes, *look up!* Look where you are going. Choose a destination — a distant tree or boathouse across the lake — and paddle toward it using the pry or J if the boat starts to wander away from your paddling side, the draw stroke if the boat wanders toward it. Yes, you'll veer and wobble around at first, but stay with it. In a short time, you'll be able to correct the boat's

direction without ever taking your eyes off your goal.

If you never learned another stroke, with these basics, you could go on great canoe adventures on lakes and easy rivers all over North America. Go on, take a leisurely paddle around the lake for a few hours before you return to your starting point and knock off for the day. In the next few sessions, we'll add a few more strokes, as well as some techniques for paddling on open water and whitewater rivers. But for now, go exploring!

✅

SKILLS CHECK

● Are you rotating your body *before* you put in the sweep, either forward or back?

● Are your hands *low*, with the paddle going out wide?

● Are you pushing *out* when you initiate the stroke?

SOLO AND CROSS BOW STROKES

Pleased with the memory of your acquisition of basic skills in a canoe and the enjoyable day you spent on the water last week, you head down to the lake again. There is much more to be learned on flat water; however, your partner can't join you until the afternoon. Fine. You can use the morning to develop some skills in paddling the boat by yourself. You can begin to master the family of solo strokes and the cross box strokes, a group of moves used by solo and bow paddlers who want to experience the thrill of manuevering down swift water.

Onto the Water

Here you are, the canoe bobbing alongside the shore waiting for your entrance. Where to sit, or, I should say, kneel? If your canoe is well outfitted for whitewater use, it will be clear from the placement of knee pads which way to get in and face when alone. But in an unadorned canoe, only the thwarts tell you. Remember that the bow seat is farther from its end of the canoe than the stern seat is. If your canoe has only these thwarts, the proper solo position is kneeling facing the stern, with your bottom resting against the bow thwart. If your canoe has a thwart directly amidships, don't be fooled; this is the portage thwart, designed to rest against your shoul-

Solo Forward Sweep

Solo Reverse Sweep

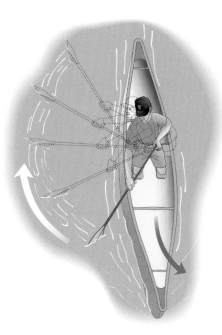

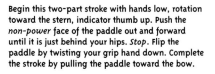

Keep hands low, indicator thumb pointed up. Push out with both hands to sweep a wide arch. Now keep sweeping *beyond* your hips, creating a nearly 180-degree arch and pulling the paddle toward the back of the canoe.

Begin this two-part stroke with hands low, rotation toward the stern, indicator thumb up. Push the *non-power* face of the paddle out and forward until it is just behind your hips. *Stop.* Flip the paddle by twisting your grip hand down. Complete the stroke by pulling the paddle toward the bow.

ders when you carry the canoe. You don't want to kneel there anyway, because that position would put you off center in the boat. As a solo paddler, you want to be paddling at the boat's pivot point, or midpoint, and to do that, you need to be sitting slightly behind that point.

In solo canoeing, you're steering the boat from its center, not from either end as with tandem canoeing. Therefore, keep in mind that you'll need to extend your strokes well in front of and behind your body. You

have a lot more boat to control there. Let's start with the sweeps and draws.

SOLO SWEEPS
Forward Sweep

Begin a solo forward sweep just as you would from the bow when canoeing tandem. Rotate forward with hands low (indicator thumb straight up), and push *out* with both hands to sweep in a wide arc that pushes the bow around. Now for the difference in the solo sweep: When the paddle reaches your body position, continue rotating rather than pulling the blade out. Keep your hands at shoulder level or below.

As your shaft hand passes your body, that arm should be comfortably extended but not locked. Keep rotating. Follow your shaft hand with your eyes and head—this will keep your body turning. As your shaft arm goes behind you, let it bend to an L shape and pull the paddle toward the side of the boat. This second half of the forward sweep is so strong that it is often used by itself. It'll even get its own name, but don't worry about that now; just try doing the stroke from as far as you can comfortably reach forward to as far as you can comfortably rotate backward. You'll feel the whole boat spinning around that magical pivot point behind which you are kneeling.

Reverse Sweep

The solo reverse sweep is a two-part stroke. You begin it just as you would a reverse sweep from the stern position when paddling tandem. Begin with rotation toward the stern and with hands low (below chest level), indicator thumb pointing up. Push the non-power face of the paddle out away from the boat until it is just slightly behind your body. *Stop.* Flip the paddle over by twisting your grip hand down, indicator thumb turning from up to down position; it should point down toward your right armpit. Now continue the stroke by pulling

Solo Standard Draw

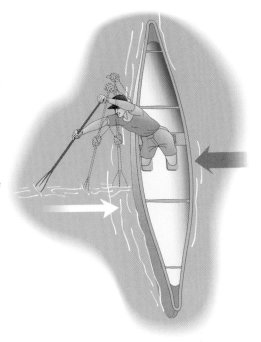

Rotate to the side, place both hands out over the water and push down with your grip hand to set the paddle blade and pull the boat toward it. When the boat gets close to the paddle, turn your indicator thumb away from the boat and slice, or feather, the blade away for another draw.

the paddle toward the bow. As you practice, you'll eliminate the stop between the phases, connecting them into one graceful stroke. However, keep them separate until you have mastered the flip of the paddle.

"Wait!" you say. "Wouldn't it be simpler to just keep going all the way to the bow with the non-power face?"

Simpler, yes, but the problem is that doing so tends to push the boat backward. You want the stroke to spin the boat around its pivot point

Solo Bow Draw

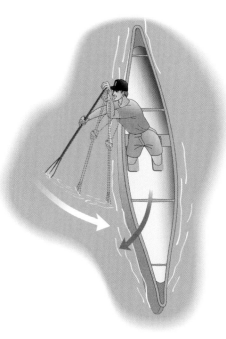

Begin as if for a standard draw, but pull the blade toward the bow. Be sure to angle the power face toward the bow, pulling the boat toward the paddle.

and then pull it in the new direction you've chosen. Many novice solo canoeists use turning strokes that slow them down, but you will not, thanks to gaining competence in combination strokes from the start. Trust me: The time spent on this now will translate into better control on rivers later on.

SOLO DRAWS
Standard Draw
A standard solo draw is identical to a tandem bow draw: Rotate to the side

Solo Stern Draw

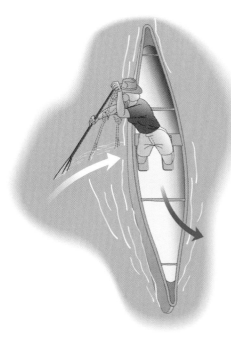

With hands at shoulder level, execute the second half of a solo forward sweep. Reach out to your side as far as you comfortably can to place the blade in the water. Now rotate back, looking down the shoulder of your shaft arm and pulling the power face toward the stern.

first, then place both hands out over the water, and push down with the grip hand to "set" the paddle blade and pull the boat toward it. When the paddle gets close to the boat, turn the indicator thumb out away from the boat, and you'll be able to slice the paddle out through the water for another stroke. For the solo boater, there are two other kinds of draws: bow and stern.

Bow Draw
In the solo bow draw, you begin as if

for a tandem bow draw, but you pull
the power face toward the bow, rather
than directly toward yourself. What's
important is that the power face of the
paddle is angled forward in the direction of the bow. Note that your indicator thumb is pointing down and
back at a slight angle and that your
shaft arm is slightly bent. Use the
rotational power of your stomach and
back muscles to pull the boat to the
paddle. Many people move the paddle
through the water too fast, wasting the
planted power of the stroke.

Stern Draw

The stern draw is used all the time
in solo boating. If the boat is
veering toward your paddling side,
you can "catch" it with a stern
draw. Here's how: Keeping your
hands about shoulder level, execute
the second half of a solo forward
sweep. Put the paddle straight out
to the side as far away from the boat
as balance and comfort allow, with
your shaft arm fully extended. If you
are paddling on the right, this
means that your right arm will be
almost fully extended out to the side
of the canoe. Your grip (left) hand,
with indicator thumb up, should be
directly above the canoe's right gunwale. Now rotate back, looking
down the shoulder of your shaft arm
and pulling the power face toward
the stern.

When the stroke is finished, the
power face of the paddle will almost
touch the stern. Properly done, this

Solo Hanging Draw (Duffek)

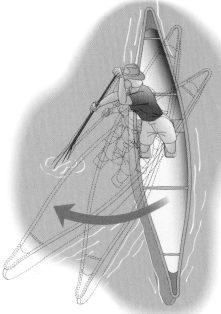

This stroke only works when there is good
current or your canoe has strong forward
momentum. Rotate toward your on-side as if for
a standard draw, but let the elbow of your
shaft-arm drop into a relaxed L, with your
upper arm almost at your side and your forearm
perpendicular to the canoe and extended out
over the water. Plant the paddle in the water
and hold that position. The boat will pivot
around the paddle.

will become one of the most useful
strokes in your solo repertoire, with
many applications that will be
described later. Its most immediate
use will be to help you keep the
boat moving along in a straight line.

Hanging Draw, or Duffek

This elegant stroke was originated in
the 1950s by Czech kayak slalom
racer Milovan Duffek, who used it to

Solo Stern Pry

As the paddle comes past your knees, rotate toward your side, drop your hands so the shaft hand is resting on the gunwale and the grip hand is at chest level, indicator thumb up. To check the off-side swing of the canoe, pull your grip hand in over the boat a few inches. Don't move your shaft hand.

pivot his boat smartly around in a single stroke. It works even better in a canoe, because the canoeist's body is freer to move within the boat, allowing better rotation and a paddle that is planted vertically in the water. The stroke neatly converts forward speed into a quick turn. It can be done only when there is water resistance against the paddle, created either by the forward speed

you provide on a lake or by the current flowing against the blade on a river. Hanging draw means just that: You place the paddle in the water, and let the boat turn around it, rather than move the blade toward the boat.

Rotate toward your on-side as if you were going to reach out and do a normal draw. This time, however, let the elbow of your shaft-hand arm drop into a relaxed L-shape, with your upper arm almost at your side and your forearm perpendicular to the canoe and extended out over the water. Plant the paddle in the water and hold that position. Does the boat move? Not at all. Not unless you are moving forward. Once you are comfortable with the motion of the stroke, get your canoe up to speed with a few strokes, rotate, and plant the paddle. Count to three: You will feel the boat swing around toward your side. When you have turned as far as you want to go, simply roll the knuckles of *both* hands toward the bow. The paddle blade will then be ready for a forward stroke, which you can take to propel yourself off in your new direction.

With the strokes you now have under your belt you are able to turn the boat reasonably well in either direction. Now you want to go somewhere. Time to paddle away into the

Solo J Stroke

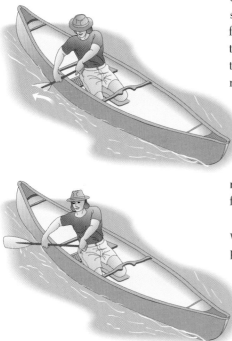

Shift to the more subtle J stroke once you have gained forward momentum. As the paddle passes your hips, turn your indicator thumb *down* so that the knuckles of both hands face the water. To make the correction, push the bent wrist of your shaft hand away from the boat.

distance using the same correctional strokes you used while tandem canoeing from the stern: the pry and the J stroke.

SOLO CORRECTION STROKES

Paddling solo, the canoe wants to jump toward your off-side the moment you take a forward stroke. You don't have a bow partner pad-dling on the other side to offset that off-side turn. The bane of beginning solo paddlers is that the boat spins so far from their side that they think they must use a strong reverse sweep to bring it back in line. But the reverse sweep kills most of the forward momentum they've gained, so back and forth they go, from forward stroke to reverse sweep. Before long, they are either weeping in frustration or are merely switching sides for several forward strokes at a time.

To avoid this scenario, begin with the canoe pointing *toward* your paddling side. If your destination is the tree across the lake at 12:00 and you are paddling on the right side, just give a bit of a bow draw until the boat is pointing at about 2:00. (It is possible, in this age of digital watches, that those instructions may be meaningless. The numbers represent the positions of the hours on an analog clock face, with 12:00 being straight ahead, 6:00 straight behind, and 3:00 and 9:00 at 90 degrees to the right and left, respectively.) Now, take a smooth, but not violent, forward stroke. The moment your paddle pushes down into the water, your bow will swing toward your off-side. To stop the swing, let your first correction stroke be a stern pry.

Stern Pry

As the paddle comes past your knees, keep rotating toward your side, let your hands drop down so that the shaft hand is resting on the gunwale and the grip hand is about chest level, indicator thumb pointing up. To stop the off-side swing, pull your grip hand in over the boat a few inches. Your shaft hand *does not move*. The leverage of the pry brings the bow back toward your paddling side smartly, and you are ready to take the next forward stroke. The canoe will already have started to glide forward.

J Stroke

After one more forward stroke and pry combination, you can shift to the J stroke, where your indicator thumb turns down and the corrective action is smaller. Practice the pry and the J stroke for as long as it takes to feel comfortable with them; they are key to precisely handling a canoe. In an hour

FOR THE BOW AND SOLO PADDLER ONLY

Cross bow moves are for solo and tandem bow paddlers only. Stern paddlers never do cross bow moves. The strokes lose their effectiveness when you try to do them from so far behind the pivot point of the canoe, and the sudden shift of weight to the same side as the bow paddler can tip you over.

or so of steady practice, you'll be able to start the boat from a dead stop, get it up to cruising speed in a few strokes, and head straight toward any destination on the lake you choose.

Why make such a fuss over this? Because many canoeists — even many who have run quite a few rivers — have not perfected the combination of a decisive forward stroke followed by an equally decisive quick pry or J stroke. Consequently, most solo canoeists I have seen, particularly in white water, have difficulty driving their canoe where they want it to go, especially when they have to change direction suddenly and then need to get back up to speed. Mastering these strokes on a lake will give you immeasurably better control on moving water and when you're paddling against head winds on flat water.

CROSS BOW STROKES

You could paddle for the rest of your life on lakes and never need the set of strokes I am about to describe. But if you plan on maneuvering in your canoe, whether it be down rapids or through the surprisingly swift current threading through a mangrove swamp, you will need to be able to turn the boat quickly to your off-side — the side on which you are not forward paddling. Forward sweeps, as you recall, will turn your boat toward your off-side, but only in a wide arc, carrying lots of speed.

"Well, why can't I just switch

Cross Bow Sweep

With your indicator thumb pointed *up*, rotate as far as is comfortable to your left. Your grip hand is at your left shoulder, and your right arm is almost fully extended out over the water on the left side of the boat. Drop the blade into the water and unwind, pulling all the way to the bow. Now pick the blade up out of the water and over the bow, put it back into the water on the right side, and continue to unwind in a forward sweep.

sides?" you ask.

Switching sides has its place in canoeing, but not for quick changes in direction. It's hard to let go of the paddle, change sides, and quickly execute an effective turning stroke with your grip and shaft hands reversed. We just aren't wired that way: Too much gets confused in the

sudden change, and your attempted strokes are likely to be clumsy and inefficient. There is a better way, and it involves an elegant use of all the rotational power in your body. In fact, once you learn the cross bows, you will want to do them for the pure pleasure of it.

Simply put, cross bow strokes involve picking your paddle up, lifting it over and across the bow, and using it on the other side of the boat.

"Isn't that the same as switching sides?"

No. When you switch sides, your grip and shaft hands exchange positions on the paddle. When you execute a cross bow, your hands stay in the same places, which means that you keep the same points of reference on the paddle. There is no confusion about your hands being reversed. Here's how to do them.

Cross Bow Sweep

All the cross bow strokes are built on the cross bow sweep. Assume you prefer paddling on the right side of the boat. Start with both arms bent at

Cross Bow Draw

Set up as if for an on-side draw, but allow your grip hand to move out over the water with your indicator thumb level and pointing toward the bow. The paddle is vertical. Now pull the paddle toward the boat. When it reaches the side, either feather the blade back for another draw, or remove the paddle by lifting your shaft arm up and forward to slice the blade out. This will bring your indicator thumb *up*.

the elbows and the indicator thumb of the grip hand pointing up. Start rotating to your left, keeping your left arm bent and relaxed while reaching across your body with your right arm, extending it as you go. Twist as far to the left as you feel comfortable. For most folks, the shaft hand will tend to rise to about shoulder level as they twist. This is fine. Once you have twisted about as far as you can go, you are wound up like a big spring full of power. Your grip hand, indicator thumb still up, is at your left shoulder, and your right arm is almost fully extended out over the water on the left side of the boat. The canoe shouldn't feel tippy because you aren't leaning out over the water: You're simply rotated as far to the left as you can.

Now drop the blade of your paddle down into the water and unwind, pulling all the way to the

TECHNIQUE TIP

TROUBLESHOOTING THE CROSS BOW SWEEP

● Don't do too many of them in a row. The cross bow sweep works best as a single powerful stroke with which to initiate a turn. If you follow it with a second or third, the momentum of the boat toward the off-side can trap your paddle against the bow, leading to comical spills (at least, comical for those watching you).

● If you don't rotate well to your off-side, you can get some extra reach by sliding your shaft hand up the shaft once you've twisted as far as you can. This will allow you to get the extra leverage that your body won't provide. But remember to slide the shaft hand back to its proper position when you return to your regular paddling side.

Cross Forward Stroke

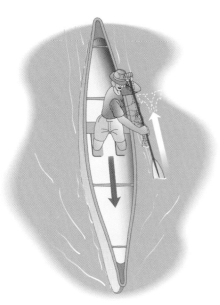

This stroke is often used to stop an off-side turn and get the boat moving straight ahead again. To execute it, complete the first half of a cross bow sweep to the point just after you pull the paddle out of the water to lift it over the bow. Instead of lifting it over the bow, turn your grip hand so that your indicator thumb points toward your ear, turning the blade in preparation for an off-side forward stroke. Now extend your grip hand forward and push down to take the off-side forward stroke. Turn to page 76 for the feathering recovery to this stroke.

bow. When you get there, pick up the paddle, put it in on the right side, and continue to unwind all the way around in what you already know as the forward sweep. Remember, the grip-hand indicator thumb stays up the whole time. Move through the entire stroke slowly so that you feel the full application of power throughout.

The cross bow sweep works so well that it is rarely necessary to add to the turn by continuing the sweep once you have lifted the paddle back over the bow to your normal paddling side, though that is still the best way to learn the full stroke and its turning power. Get comfortable with the full stroke; practice it often. In no time, you'll be able to turn the canoe 180 degrees in a single stroke to the off-side. Because of the automatic rotation that comes with it, you'll find the off-side phase of the cross bow strokes to be more powerful than the on-side turning strokes.

Now that you can handle basic

TECHNIQUE TIP

TROUBLESHOOTING THE CROSS FORWARD STROKE

● Keep it short. The value of the stroke is lost almost at once after you have pushed the blade down in the water at the moment of catch.

● Learn to feather the paddle out forward.

● Practice this seemingly complicated stroke. Once you become fluent in it, you can use it anytime you need a forward "push" on your off-side; you won't need to use it only for stopping the movement of a cross bow sweep.

Feathering Recovery

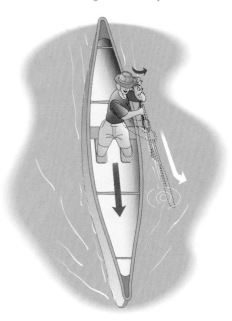

To get the paddle out of the water after a cross forward stroke, twist your grip hand so that your indicator thumb faces forward. Now lift your shaft hand up and forward to slice the blade out of the water. Be sure to execute this move while your paddle is still out in front of you; if you wait until it's back as far as your hips, your arms will become tied in knots.

cross bow moves, there is still time to learn a few snazzy ones before your tandem partner arrives.

Cross Bow Draw

Sometimes, you simply want to yank the boat sideways. You already know how to do that on your paddling side with the draw. Now you want the same effect on your off-side. Set up as you would for the cross bow sweep, but this time, instead of keeping the grip hand close to your body and your

indicator thumb up, allow the grip hand to move out over the water with the indicator thumb level and pointing toward the bow. The paddle is vertical, just as it is for an on-side draw. Now pull the paddle toward the boat. The problem most people encounter is getting the cross draw out of the water. If it comes in all the way to the boat, the paddle blade is likely to get stuck against the hull, levering you out and causing your surprised face to be the first thing into the water. You need to feather your paddle blade back out for another draw or simply to remove the paddle. To do so, lift your shaft hand up and forward to slice the blade the same way. This will bring the indicator thumb *up* and leave you in a position almost identical to the end of a cross bow sweep's first phase.

Cross Forward Stroke

As you have found, the cross bow sweep turns you amazingly well toward your off-side — sometimes too well. Novice solo paddlers often find that the stroke sets up so much turning momentum that when they go back to take a forward stroke on their regular paddling side, the canoe keeps turning away from them — like the frustrating period when they were trying to go straight! The cross forward stroke is the best response. Here's how it works.

Follow the same process that you would to take a cross bow sweep. Complete the first half of the stroke to just after you lift the paddle out of the water to lift it over the bow. Don't lift it over the bow. Instead, turn your grip hand so that the indicator thumb is pointing toward your ear. This turns the paddle blade so that it is set up for a forward stroke on your off-side.

Now extend your grip hand forward, and push down to take a forward stroke on your off-side. Notice how the canoe stopped turning toward that side and began to move forward? That's what the stroke is often used for: to stop an off-side turn and get moving forward again.

FEATHERING RECOVERY. To get the paddle out of the water after a cross forward stroke, twist your grip hand so that your indicator thumb faces forward. Now all you have to do is lift your shaft hand up and forward to slice the blade of the paddle out of the water. This will bring the indicator thumb *up* and leave you in a position almost identical to the end of a cross bow sweep's first phase. This elegant recovery must *always* be executed while the paddle is still out in front of you. If you let the paddle come back — even as far as your hips — you'll find your arms getting tied in knots.

On a lake, the cross forward is of limited use, but there will come a time soon on your river explorations when you will be very glad you know it.

HONING YOUR SKILLS

You have all the strokes that you need for a lifetime of canoeing. Now it is a matter of practicing them so that your execution is the same in all conditions. There are a few more advanced strokes — such as the Reverse J, which allows you to go backward at speed — but they are beyond the scope of this book. For the most part, advanced strokes in canoeing are not so much new strokes as they are unusual combinations of standard strokes instantly improvised to meet a need. You don't have to worry about that for some time.

After a morning of practice, some frustration, and much success, you are ready to take a lunch break. You paddle — in a respectably straight line — alone and unaided, back to the dock where you began. Just short of your landing spot, you do a reverse sweep, then slow the turn down by drawing gently. The canoe obediently swings sideways and, slowed by your draw strokes, lightly touches the dock. Your timing has been perfect: All this control has been performed under the impressed gaze of your paddling partner, who has stopped to watch as she lugs a well-stocked picnic basket down to the water's edge.

"Wow! You've gotten a lot better!"

"Yeah," you reply with suitable modesty, "but it won't take you long." You explain to your friend what she will need to learn about off-side moves: cross draws and the like, gesturing in the air with your grip hand, indicator thumb precisely showing the way.

"After lunch, we can practice all this with some landing drills."

"Landing drills?"

Landing Drills

The only problem with learning the control strokes of canoeing on a lake is that there is very little immediate need for precise control. After all, there is plenty of room. What's the hurry to turn on a dime?

It is precisely this reasoning that causes so many canoeists to get stuck at a fairly low level of control: They

Landing Drills

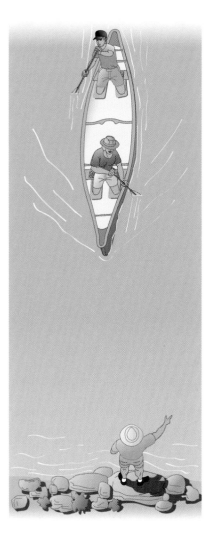

With a friend on shore to direct you, paddle directly toward shore from about 50 yards out. The person on shore waits until you are about 50 feet from shore before signaling which way you must turn. You then turn in that direction (smartly, it is hoped), stop the boat, and bring it in sideways to lightly touch the shore. Repeat the process, both picking up more speed on the way toward shore, and having your friend wait later to signal which direction you should turn. Be sure to practice turns in either direction; most paddlers turn more naturally to one side than the other.

don't see the need for working on more. That attitude works well enough until they get into a situation where they do need control, such as when they go paddling on an "easy" little stream and discover that moving water takes them quickly to places they might not want to go. Look ahead to the adventures you will have, and prepare for them by making up obstacles and exercises on the lake where you are learning. In addition to the techniques you are perfecting, you'll find that you are gaining canoe-specific fitness. Here is one of the simplest and best drills that can be applied anywhere.

To do this drill, you need one person on shore (or on a dock) directing one or more canoeists. The canoes, whether occupied by pairs or individuals, start from about 50 yards out and paddle steadily in, aiming directly at the person on shore. Don't go fast at first; just maintain a steady rate of speed. The person on shore waits until the canoe is about 50 feet

away and then points either left or right. The canoeist(s) then turn in the indicated direction, stop the boat, and then bring it in sideways to lightly touch the shore (or dock). Landings do not have to be done toward land. You can do this same exercise aiming at each other: one person in a stationary boat giving directions to other canoes coming in at a right angle to the stationary boat.

Landing drills are useful for everyone, regardless of skill or experience. In tandem teams, they promote the unquestioning and immediate taking of complementary strokes, the stern person following the bow's lead. In bow paddlers and solo boaters, they promote the quick reaction time between recognizing the need to turn and the execution of the correct turn. Done properly and slowly, landings are also a great place to teach your bow partner the off-side strokes.

As your skill increases, so can your approach speed, with less warning time given for the turns.

Accomplished paddlers can do this exercise from full speed to a complete stop within the length of the canoe. The point, of course, is to apply in shorter and shorter chunks of time the strokes you have learned. The immediacy of reaction this exercise gives will help immeasurably when you venture onto rivers with current. Landings are meant to be fun, so they should be paced according to the skills of the participants.

Shoreline Skimming

An excellent way to hone skills that beautifully simulates the kind of maneuvering required in rapids is to deliberately stay close to the shoreline of a lake. Aim to hug the shoreline for hundreds of yards at a time, veering out as necessary to avoid docks, downed trees, branches, submerged boulders, and other obstacles. Keep your boat within 2 feet of shore, and work on maintaining a constant speed. Change directions periodically — or hug the opposite bank — to allow each paddler the opportunity to take strokes in the limited space between boat and shore. This exercise will force you to focus on your strokes and give you instant feedback if you take them improperly.

Obstacle Courses

Even better, if you can find them, are courses that force you to move *around* obstacles, such as moored boats. Again, stay as close as possible to the obstacles and maintain a constant speed.

Such drills teach you precise maneuvering in situations where there is little or no stress so that you are able to function when there might be more. So go on, add a little spice to paddling around the lake. Dodge around the big sycamore tree leaning out over the water, and paddle in tight patterns around the moored boats at the summer camp at the end of the lake. But remember, when you tire of the drills, stop. Paddle off down the lake with your partner or alone. Revel in what you've learned, and plan in your mind the camping trip next weekend on a lake not too far — but far enough — from town.

C A M P I N G
B Y
C A N O E

L akes, even well-known ones, constitute blanks on the maps. There are no contour lines, just wide-open blue spaces that beg you to explore them — shallow marshes where motorboats can't go; archipelagos of spruce-topped ledges on which to snack, doze, or camp; and narrow inlets where creeks enter in small falls. Your canoe is designed for just this sort of exploration, and it's toward this end that you have spent so much time paddling in circles, building your skills. And canoes are worthy carriers of gear and people on long trips. One friend of mine went with a team on a 60-day adventure into the Canadian Arctic completely self-contained — no resupply points en route. An overnight trip will require that you carry much of the same basic gear that my friend carried: after clothes and shelter, most additional weight on long trips is composed of food.

On a first overnight trip, you want to test organization, skills, and gear in friendly surroundings, learning first-hand just what a great vehicle of exploration the canoe is. But before you go, be aware that just because a lake is flat doesn't mean paddling across it is without hazards. In fact, most canoeing accidents occur on lakes — not rivers — often because people, assuming that nothing will go wrong, take inadequate precautions.

So by all means go, but for your first canoe camping venture, stick to a benign local lake. Think of it as a test cruise to try out all your systems and skills, from deciding how to dress and what to bring to playing out a few "could-have-been" emergency scenarios.

Lake canoeing and camping is about general aware-ness. There are few technical strokes to remember, because all you do is paddle your boat across open water to your desired destination, haul the packed gear out of the boats, and set up camp. Much of this chapter is about the gear and preparations for such a trip, but I will spend some time detailing the self-rescue skills you'll need to practice.

WHAT TO BRING

Camping in a canoe may perma-nently ruin traditional backpacking for you, because you can carry so much with ease. Still, there are some limitations to what you can carry, depending on the sort of trip you have in mind. And the way in which you pack and stow all that delicious food and luxurious gear can make all the difference.

Pack what you would take with you on any overnight camping trip: food, tent or tarp, change of clothes, and safety gear (see *Hiking & Back-packing*, a Trailside Series guide, for details). While you don't have to fuss over space and weight control with the precision of a backpacker, remember that if you plan to carry the canoe and its load overland from one lake to another nearby, a process called portaging, pack sen-sibly enough that your gear can be carried in a fairly compact and trans-portable bundle. A tandem team of canoeists can carry all their food and camping gear for an overnight trip in two packs each about the size of a standard duffel bag: 3 feet long and 1 1/2 feet high. Here's a checklist to follow for your first overnight foray, with some specific recommendations for a canoeist's needs.

Food
Because of the generous carrying capacity of the canoe, you can bring bulkier foods than a backpacker would be willing (or able) to carry, so indulge yourself with loaves of

good bread, salads, plenty of fresh fruit, meat, even desert. All this should be stored in bombproof containers, either of the Tupperware variety or the thickest plastic bags you can find, double-layered for good measure. For your first camping trip, prepare a favorite meal at home, be it chili, spaghetti, or coq au vin, then freeze and bag it and take it along. Or just throw in porterhouse steaks if a campfire is allowed. And don't stint on breakfast; there's plenty of room to stash pre-mixed pancake batter, eggs, bacon, the works. You'll have enough other new experiences to deal with, so you might as well make your food preparation simple and your meal rewarding. Store various ingredients separately in trash compactor bags. These extremely heavy plastic bags are almost guaranteed to hold up to all the abuse you can provide.

While canoeing may not be as rigorous as backpacking, being out under the sky and on the water all day — to say nothing of paddling across a lake against even a modest

headwind — will burn through loads of calories. So bring snacks that pack a caloric punch, such as dried fruits, nuts, chocolate, candy bars, fresh fruit and granola.

Assuming you are paddling on fresh water and not salt, there is an obvious abundance of the stuff. Sadly, however, there is almost no body of water on earth from which it is safe to drink, either due to pollutants or the presence of bacteria or parasites. Bring a good water-purifying filtration system (see Sources & Resources at the back of the book), or be prepared to flavor your coffee with iodine or other chemicals to kill the nasty microscopic inhabitants that may lurk in the water.

Cooking Gear

Environmental sensitivity and convenience demand that you take along a camping stove. Fires, although very satisfying, are a hazard in dry weather, can be difficult to start in wet conditions, and in any event are

You can't count on being allowed to light campfires, and in many areas doing so is ill-advised even if not officially banned. An efficient back-packing stove like these lightweight models is one answer, though when canoe camping you may allow yourself the luxury of a larger Coleman-style two-burner camp stove.

An old-style canoe camp on the banks of the Smith River in Montana near the river's confluence with the Missouri.

prohibited in more and more areas of the country. And unless you take great pains to remove all evidence of them, campfires scar campsites; they are best reserved for sites where permanent firepits or grills are provided. If you own a Coleman-style two-burner camp stove, another luxury allowed canoe campers, it will serve nicely. If you are in the market for a stove, consider one of the many excellent portable models. They range in price from $40 to more than $100 and will also serve you well on backpacking adventures. Nesting pots allow you to carry a small coffeepot, a frying pan, and a second pot inside a single gallon container.

Toilet Gear

It is essential that every group going into the backcountry know how to dispose of their own waste in a hygienic and ecologically sound manner (described on page 96). For your toilet kit, you need a gardening trowel, toilet paper, and several sets of standard zip-lock plastic kitchen bags for disposing of paper.

Shelter

Any three-season backpacking tent or tarp will do fine. Tarps are appealing because of their simplicity and light weight, but they don't offer insect protection. In buggy country (and this includes much of the prime canoeing waters of the northern United States and Canada during most of the canoeable weather), the insect netting on a well-made tent might be the only thing between you and the loss of sanity caused by repeated insect bites. (See *Hiking & Backpacking*, a Trailside Series guide, for advice on which tent to buy.)

Clothing

Nowadays, there is no excuse not to layer yourself with one or all of the "miracle fiber" group of synthetic fabrics: polyester, Capilene, and nylon. They are available everywhere and are priced to match any budget. All of them dry extremely quickly and provide some warmth even when wet. Always pack several layers rather than one bulky garment. Use these — from the thinnest fabric closest to your skin to the thickest as a final layer — along with a water- and wind-resistant shell garment to complete your system. Here is a complete wardrobe that will handle temperatures from freezing up into the 80s:

- water-sports shoes or sandals (i.e., footwear that can get wet)
- 1 pair nylon shorts
- 2 pairs wool or synthetic socks
- 1 set lightweight synthetic underwear, tops and long johns
- 1 pair medium-weight long johns
- 1 synthetic pile jacket
- 1 synthetic or wool hat
- 1 pair wool or synthetic gloves
- 1 paddling shell garment: pants and a jacket.

Paddling shell gear is of wind- and water-resistant material like rain gear, but it is cut to allow unhindered paddling. Do not wear a poncho or bulky rain jacket; they can dangerously burden you in the event of a swim.

All of the above-mentioned gear is lightweight and takes up little room. It protects you in a wide range of temperatures, accommodating expeditions during all seasons but winter in most North American canoeing areas. If you wore everything on the list, you would be warm in quite chilly conditions. On sunny days when the temperature warms up, you would remove layers of clothing until you were clad only in the shorts. This list is a basic minimum. Anything else you carry is up to you.

Safety Gear

For lake canoeing, this includes:
- Your PFD (see Chapter 1 for details) — Take it! Whether you wear it is up to you, but it should be immediately available at all times and worn during open-water crossings and whenever you are more than 100 yards from shore.
- First Aid Kit — This can be amended to the needs of the party and the duration of the trip, but you should always have the basic necessities of sunscreen, bandages, anti-inflammatories such as aspirin or ibuprofen, and dressings to control bleeding. To the surprise of many people, excellent first aid can be rigged from improvised materials; training is far more important than a fancy kit.

If you are going to spend any time in a place where there is no easy access to professional medical help, you must acquire first aid training. Call your local American Red Cross chapter for information on courses near you, and take one.

The subject of first aid requires detailed instruction and is beyond the scope of this book. (See Sources & Resources for recommended reading.)

All backcountry travelers should also familiarize themselves with what to do in the case of a severe allergic reaction. There is, in fact, only one adequate response: the Ana-kit or Epi-pen injectable epinephrine kits. In most states, a

☑

CLOTHING CHECKLIST

Here is a complete wardrobe that will handle temperatures from freezing up into the 80s:

- water sports shoes or sandals (*i.e.*: footwear that can get wet)
- 1 pair nylon shorts
- 2 pairs wool or synthetic socks
- 1 set lightweight synthetic underwear, tops and long johns
- 1 pair medium weight long johns
- 1 synthetic pile jacket
- 1 synthetic or wool hat
- 1 pair wool or synthetic gloves
- 1 paddling shell garment: pants and a jacket.

three-hour course certifies you to administer a dose of these drugs. In a severe allergic reaction, doing so could very well save a life.

Rope

While rope is not as frequently used for safety on lake trips as it is in whitewater, it's wise to have at least 50 feet of stout (at least 3/8-inch-diameter) polypropylene rope. Specify poly: It floats, while most nylon rope does not. A 50-foot length of rope is a must if you encounter a place to "line" your boat around rapids you don't care to run (see Chapter 9, page 166) and has a variety of other uses, from tying canoes to shore to rigging a line to keep food bags in the air and out of reach of varmints like raccoons and bears.

The Canoe

For the kind of outing you have in mind, the same sturdy general-purpose boat in which you learned your strokes will do fine. This is not the place to get into all the designs available for flatwater paddling. If you find that going on extended trips across lakes is your favored form of canoeing, you'll soon get a specialized boat that is fairly long, tracks well in a straight line, and accommodates plenty of gear.

Paddles

Take your standard paddle, and bring a spare paddle for each canoe on the trip.

PACKING & LOADING

Canoes can carry a great deal of extra weight (up to 1,000 pounds), but you can't be cavalier about haphazardly throwing duffels on board. You want the load kept as low as possible in the boat and stored in the center — right at the widest point amidships. If paddling tandem, you want to store the packs here to avoid changing the trim of the boat — the weight should settle the boat evenly in the water without making the bow or stern dip more — affecting the canoe's handling. If paddling alone, move the packs forward so that the boat floats level or even with a slightly heavy bow. This way, when you paddle forward, the boat will plane. If you have too much weight toward the stern, the boat will "squat" with the bow high, causing it to slow down and handle poorly.

Packs

The traditional pack of canoe travel is the Duluth, a large squared-off duffel bag with shoulder straps attached. Duluth packs are made of heavy cotton and last forever. Traditionalists love to stuff these monsters with gear and carry them with a tumpline, an ancient method of carrying loads. The tumpline runs under the bag and around your forehead; no shoulder straps, just neck and back muscles twanging. It is as bad as it sounds. Devotees of the Duluth pack then stagger around bellowing old French-Canadian voyageur songs. If you go

Safety and comfort in a canoe: two life jackets, one to wear and one to snooze on. Canoe camping is for all ages, as this child on Follensby Clear Pond in Adirondack State Park, New York, proves.

this route, be fully traditional: Take several casks of rum to ease the pain.

Modern canoe packs look similar but are made of waterproof fabrics like vinyl or rubberized nylon. Any duffel bag or internal frame backpack will do for the occasional canoe camping trip. What really matters is lining the pack with a heavy plastic trash bag *and* individually bagging clothes, gear, and food in zip-lock or plastic garbage bags within the pack.

A canoe laden well over the gunwales with gear lashed in with bungee cords is pulled ashore along Forty Mile River in Alaska. Canoes designed for long trips can carry upwards of 1,000 pounds.

lock bags of gear.

To seal a trash bag, be sure to fill it only about two-thirds full. This leaves you plenty of room to close the top and twist at least a foot-long neck onto it. You can then tie this neck with a simple overhand knot, leaving the tail sticking out to make untying easier. Although waterproof, trash bags

Water gets in everywhere, but carefully double-bagging everything works well.

You can buy heavy-duty river duffels with waterproof zippers, but they are expensive and water seems to find its way even into those. A reasonably priced compromise is the Boundary Bag made by Cascade Designs, which is made of durable waterproof fabric, has straps and a watertight rolltop closure and costs $10 to $50, depending on size. But remember: Any bag can be made watertight and will float indefinitely if it is lined with a trash bag and contains other sealed trash or zip-

tear easily. Take many spares with you; they have scores of uses and are lightweight.

Lashing in the Gear
What about lashing all those waterproof containers into the canoe in case of a flip? There are two schools of thought on this. In one, all the gear

is lashed in tightly so that there is no way it can shift at all. In the other, a single line laced through the packs' handles attaches them to the canoe at only one point — usually one of the thwarts. Although it seems to go against common sense, I prefer the second method for lake travel. There is no need for tight lashing as long

This 16-1/2 foot Mad River Malecite canoe can accommodate 850 pounds, making it suited to short camping trips. To minimize the effects of wind on open water, its profile has been kept low at bow and stern. The flared bow — the hull is slightly asymmetrical — allows this canoe to rise over waves rather than driving through them. The optional center seat lets this model double as a solo canoe.

lashed in makes gun-wale-over-gunwale rescues improbable indeed.

as the packs fit fairly snugly in the boat. The purpose of the line is to keep your gear from floating away in the event of a flip. The line should be long enough that the packs will float alongside the canoe while you empty it of water. If the packs are securely lashed in, it is very difficult to empty the boat of water without being forced to unload everything. Even in shallow water, lifting a canoe with packs in it is very difficult; having the packs

OUT ON THE WATER

Lakes, however benign they appear on a sunny summer's afternoon, do have their hazards. Alerting you to them is not meant to intimidate but to inform you. Facts don't cease to exist because they are ignored, so here are some to consider as you move out onto the water.

You have waterproofed and packed all your gear, lashed it into the boat, and gotten your partner in as well. For safety and company, there are three other voyageurs joining you in two other canoes, one tandem and one solo. On your first

The larger the lake, the more powerful the effect of wind and waves, and the more important to resist the urge to cut across open bays to save time. It's best to stay within swimmable distance of shore, where the sheltering land cuts down on wind.

trip, don't try to cover too much distance. A steady but not exhausting paddling pace is about equivalent to a walking pace: 2 to 4 miles an hour. For most of your trip, you should be following shoreline, staying within several hundred yards of land.

Open-Water Crossings

An open-water crossing is one that takes you more than a quarter mile from shore and should not be taken lightly. The bigger the body of water, the more powerful the effect of wind and waves and the more difficult it

> 66 Of what use are forty freedoms without a blank spot on the map? 99
>
> — Aldo Leopold

can be to estimate from shore what the conditions in the center of the lake are — or could become. Some unnecessary tragedies have occurred with groups of canoeists who "went for it" in cutting across an open bay to shorten the distance of their trip and got into trouble far from shore. It takes a long time to cross a mile-wide neck of a lake (15 to 30 minutes), and a mile is a very long way to swim for most people — especially when they weren't planning on doing so.

To be prudent, treat open-water crossings with the same regard for safety you would for a more obviously hazardous river rapid. Always wear your PFD, and dress for a swim. If the lake is cold, you need to wear clothing that will help insulate you in the event of a spill. This is particularly true of the great northern canoeing waters, where water temperatures are low enough (below 50°F) to render a swimmer helpless after fewer than 15

PRACTICE DRILL

OPEN-WATER RESCUES

On your inaugural trip, you have paddled an easy 6 miles away from the road head following the lee shoreline. You've found the campsite you'd planned on reaching. It is only 2:00 p.m. Fine. Go ahead and set up camp, then practice some rescue drills in the warmth of the afternoon. After you have unloaded your packs and set up tents, put on your PFDs, go back to your canoes, and paddle a few yards offshore into deep water. Go through the following *one boat at a time*:

● Jump out of your canoe. If paddling tandem, both of you jump out. Now try to get back in without flipping the canoe. This requires you to climb in opposite each other on opposite sides and ends of the canoe. If you cannot do this unsupported, get the upright canoeists to paddle over and stabilize your canoe while you get in.

● Flip, and get back into the swamped canoe. This may seem silly, but it is a more protected place and allows you to retain some warmth. The practice is good just to get a feel for the stability of the canoe in this position. Besides, in a worst-case situation — in the water far from shore — it's safest to stay with your boat and move as little as possible to conserve as much body heat as possible. Remember, however, that such scenarios are best avoided by exercising good conservative judgment.

● After you have floated in the swamped canoe, get out and try emptying it as best you can using the method described on page 43.

● Have the two upright canoes "raft up," which just means line up side by side with the paddlers holding onto the gunwales. Using this stable platform, try getting one of the swimmers out of the water and into one of the canoes while the other swimmer stays in the water and swings the end of the canoe out for a gunwale-over-gunwale rescue (see page 45 for details).

● Try the gunwale-over-gunwale rescue with just two canoes, one swamped and the other upright. See if the solo canoeist can be the rescuing boat.

This is the sequence of open-water rescues that you owe to yourself to try, and with this additional provision: The next day, when you paddle back to your starting point, try all these drills with the boats fully loaded

continued on page 92

with your gear. What do you have to risk? At worst, some of your stuff will get wet, you'll find out where your waterproofing failed, and you will have to dry everything at home. More important, you'll know exactly what it feels like to rescue a swamped and loaded canoeist. Time yourself, not as a racer, but in the interest of gathering information.

If you cannot get into an upright canoe without help, you must either practice until you can or think twice about paddling alone. If the result of these drills is that you resolve to get more physically fit or more flexible or to practice the exercises until you can do them well — fine. You are thinking ahead, visualizing your strengths and limitations; that new awareness is fundamental to a long, happy, safe canoeing career.

minutes, regardless of how warm the air might be. On all open-water crossings, it's imperative that the group of canoeists stay close to each other to effect rescues if needed.

Wind and Waves

Open water often means wind, and wind has a powerful effect on a canoe. It is extremely difficult to make headway against a mere 20-mile-an-hour wind, and such a wind can create 3-to-4-foot waves in a fairly short time. Huge lakes, such as the Great Lakes, can suddenly spawn truly oceanic conditions. Canoeists in open boats do not belong out in winds greater than Force 5 on the Beaufort Scale (see page 93). Always remain open to the graceful decision to play it safe as you learn this sport. If conditions look as if they are changing, choose the conservative

option and stay close to shore, even if it means paddling farther. If wind appears to be preventing you from reaching your planned campsite, be flexible: Choose a new site closer at hand. Experienced canoeists know that the best time to go for a big crossing is dawn, when wind currents have not yet built up in the heat of the day. They also know that there are days when it is best to remain "wind bound," to explore the shore or stay in camp and settle in with that book they brought along.

You will quickly learn the meaning of the terms windward and lee shores. The windward shore is the shore toward which the wind blows, the lee shore the one away from which it blows. The lee shore is the protected side, where the land shelters the canoeist from the force of the wind. Paddling out from the quiet zone of the lee shore into a heavy wind just once will fix this distinction in your memory.

For your part, stick close to shore, and avoid paddling on the big wind days until you have amassed enough experience (and the judgment born of that experience) to put you beyond the scope of this book.

MAKING A LAKESHORE CAMP

Securing the Boats

Stories abound of canoes being washed or blown away in the night, but canoe campers repeat these mistakes every year. Canoes are relatively light, yet have a fairly large surface area, making them perfect

BEAUFORT SCALE OF WIND SPEED

Canoeists should not be out in Force 6 or greater winds.

Beaufort Number or Force	Wind Speed			World Meteorological Organization Description	Estimating Wind Speed		
	Knots	mph	km/hr		Effects Observed at Sea	Effects Observed Near Land	Effects Observed on Land
0	under 1	under 1	under 1	Calm	Sea like a mirror	Calm	Calm; smoke rises vertically
1	1-3	1-3	1-5	Light Air	Ripples with appearances of scales; no foam crests	Small sailboat just has steerage way	Smoke drift indicates wind direction; vanes do not move
2	4-6	4-7	6-11	Light Breeze	Small wavelets; crests of glassy appearance, not breaking	Wind fills the sails of small boats which then travel about 1–2 knots	Wind felt on face; leaves rustle; vanes begin to move
3	7-10	8-12	12-19	Gentle Breeze	Large wavelets; crests begin to break, scattered whitecaps	Sailboats begin to heel and travel at about 3 – 4 knots	Leaves, small twigs in constant motion; light flags extend
4	11-16	13-18	20-28	Moderate Breeze	Small waves 0.5– 1.25 meters high becoming longer; numerous whitecaps	Good working breeze, sailboats carry all sail with good heel	Dust, leaves, and loose paper raised up; small branches move
5	17-21	19-24	29-38	Fresh Breeze	Moderate waves of 1.25 –2.5 meters taking longer form; many whitecaps; some spray	Sailboats shorten sail	Small trees in leaf begin to sway

fall of wave action can cause a canoe left partially in the water to rub repeatedly against a rock or another canoe, and I have seen even tough new plastic canoes develop badly worn spots after such a night.

An ideal canoe campsite on Upper Saranac Lake in the Adirondacks in northern New York State. Always either secure your canoe by tying it to a tree or, better, as here, by pulling it ashore.

Securing Your Food

The waters most of you are going to cover on your first canoe trips will not be true wilderness — there is very little of that anywhere — but rather beautiful and relatively unpopulated open country used for recreation by thousands of other people. Most campsites you use will have been used by many others before you, and the little creatures of the woods (and a few of the big ones) know that. Therefore, it is wise to store all of your food well away from your sleeping area, unless you like the idea of being held hostage by a belligerent skunk in search of the granola stored at your side. With one of the lengths of rope you included, hoist your food bag high into the air with a rope thrown over the limb of a nearby tree.

targets for capricious gusts of wind. On large lakes, wind can turn a mirrorlike surface into a wave-chopped sea with real surf, surf that can pull untethered canoes away. River levels rise and fall, often with no apparent relation to the weather you are experiencing: Heavy rains or a dam release upstream can cause the river to rise silently, lifting and carrying away all your boats while you and your friends are laughing about stories over dinner.

Every canoe pulled up on shore for the night must be secured in some way. The easiest is to run a length of rope under the thwarts of the canoes and secure the rope to a tree or rock. Turn the canoes over so that they will not fill with rain, and carry them fully out of the water. The gentle rise and

How to Bear-Bag

To keep your food safe from bears and other smaller mammals, find a tree with a branch about 20 feet off the ground. The ideal branch is one with little foliage that is too thin to support the weight of a bear. (Adult black bears climb trees; adult grizzlies do not.) 1) Tie a rock to the end of your rope. Hint: The thicker the rope, the less likely it is to get tangled. 2) Toss the rope over the branch. The weight of the rock should bring it down. Untie the rock and tie your food bag to the rope. Pull the food bag all the way up to the tree branch. 3) Tie a counterweight (usually another food bag) to the other side of the rope as high up on the rope as you can reach. Knot, coil, or tuck away the excess rope. Push the counterweight up with a stick or your paddle until the food bag and the counterweight are several feet below the branch and at least 10 feet off the ground.

Instead of using a counterweight, you can tie the rope off on the tree trunk. But be warned: Bears in high-use areas know all about this trick, and have learned to bite or claw through the rope.

You are sharing the woods with those who came there before and those who will come after you. The ethic of "no-impact camping" is a worthy one and is followed to commendable extremes by its advocates. Most of us, however, fall back on common sense. If you are camping in a popular area, don't try to restore your campsite to some pristine state by removing the stones from the fire circle. Recognize that others will come after you and build another circle. And don't go in search of your own pristine site. If every camper did so, larger areas of the woods would be marred. Instead, use established campsites, and concentrate your efforts on leaving nothing of your own behind in any form and leaving the site attractive for the next party. The biggest problem in popular canoe-camping areas is that of human waste. It's a concern everywhere we backpack and camp, but especially so along waterways.

Camp Toilets

Friends of mine who work for the Forest Service on the Chattooga Wild and Scenic River in South Carolina say that the improper disposal of human waste is one of the top issues contributing to the deteriorating quality of backcountry experiences for all users.

On certain desert rivers of the American Southwest, such as the Colorado River through the Grand Canyon, the landscape is so delicate that it cannot sustain all its visitors digging small personal latrines. There, campers are required to carry out all their solid waste in containers. Using portable camp toilets and the necessary disinfectants, this is not at all unpleasant and may become required in other parts of the country. It certainly is the way to register the least possible impact. Until that is required of all of us, most campers in the United States will continue to dig small personal latrines. Because most of the country has an active layer of composting topsoil, this can be eco-logically sound if you do the fol-lowing:

1. Dig your latrine at least 200 feet from any trail, campsite, or water source.
2. Using a trowel, cut out a square of topsoil about 6 inches by 6 inches, and set it aside.
3. Dig down about 6 inches.
4. Use the pit, but *do not leave toilet paper in it*. It will not degrade. Sim-plest bet, particularly on an overnight, is to have a plastic zip-lock bag into which you put used toilet paper that you carry home and then dispose of. Some people advo-

cate burning the paper down to ash, but this can be a fire hazard in dry seasons or on dry terrain and is more difficult than you think.
5. Replace all dirt in the pit, and replace the square of topsoil, tamping it down gently. Spread pine needles or leaves over the area so that your use is invisible.
6. Return to camp, and wash your hands with an antibacterial soap.

If you bury excrement in this fashion, the natural composting processes and organisms in the top-soil will reduce your waste to soil in less than a month. That's it. No big deal. In fact, you no more handle human waste and toilet paper in this process than you do in your bathroom at home, yet I've seen normally rational people come unglued at the thought of any of this. Some try the biologically challenging task of not defecating for three days, while others just secretively "break the rules" and leave their toilet paper behind. Be frank with your traveling companions at the beginning of the trip to spare yourself all this silliness.

Enough talk. You have worked pleasantly hard to get here. You and your friends have finished dinner, cleaned the dishes without using dishwashing detergent, and poured the excess water into a sump hole, rather like a latrine, far from camp, straining out any food bits and putting them in a trash bag for dis-

text continued on page 100

THE SINGULAR
ART OF PORTAGING

Portaging — the skill (or is it art? athletic event? penance?) of carrying a canoe and gear overland, has been a part of canoeing since the Native Americans first invented the craft. Its necessity, however odious, is obvious: Either you must carry the canoe around a stretch of river you choose not to paddle, or you carry it from one body of water to another, not too distant one.

Just about all the great long-distance canoe trips of the north-country — Maine, Minnesota's and Ontario's boundary waters, and all of Canada and the Arctic — require that you pick up your canoe and carry it from time to time. Portages can be simple affairs of several yards as you carry your canoe and gear around an unrunnable falls, or they can be hikes of several miles from one lake to another, or even over a mountain to reach another river flowing off its far side into another drainage. Portaging well instills a certain pride: You can't help but feel that by your effort you are separating yourself from those unwilling to go to all that bother. And you're right; the more portages there are in a canoe trip, the fewer people you are likely to see. You might as well learn to do it right. Here's how:

DIVISION OF LABOR
There are two main things to carry: the canoe, and all the gear in it. Tradition has it that — assuming you are paddling on a camping trip with at least a few partners — one person should get the canoe and one person the gear. If you prepare the canoe properly and pack your gear well, everything can be moved in one trip. There are, however, some exceptions.

SHORT PORTAGES On uneven ground or in steep terrain around a drop, keep the canoe

continued on page 98

THE ART OF PORTAGING
continued from page 97

low, Carry it with one person at bow and stern holding onto the deck plates. This way, the canoe can't fall far if you lose your footing, and it is easy to set down when you need to step over obstacles. If the portage is quite short, all members of the party might team up to move one canoe at a time. This is safe, unlikely to strain anyone, and means you can keep all the gear lashed into the canoe. With two people at the bow and two at the stern, each holding onto a thwart, the canoe can be moved efficiently. This is an effective arrangement for carries up to 50 yards or so.

LONGER CARRIES

THE CANOE. What? Carry a 17-foot 80-pound beast all by yourself? Actually, it isn't so bad. The hardest part is getting the boat up onto your shoulders and down again. If the portage path follows reasonably level ground (and I recommend that beginners stick to trips on level terrain) and is longer than 50 yards, it makes sense to turn the canoe over, pick it up, and rest its center thwart on your shoulders.

There are two ways to heft it up there. The easiest is to have other members of the party pick up the canoe so that you can position yourself beneath it. Or, as described on page 31, you can turn the boat over and work your way backwards from one end until it is resting on your shoulders.

Remember, the center thwart allows you to balance the boat quite nicely on your shoulders. In canoes designed for long trips, the center thwart is shaped like a yoke to fit the back of your neck and shoulders comfortably.

For carries up to about 200 yards, your PFD will provide sufficient padding. On longer carries, tie two paddles lengthwise about shoulder width apart between the bow and the portage thwarts, and pad the paddle shafts with clothing or PFDs. This setup is very comfortable and the method of choice on longer hauls.

If you can't carry a canoe by yourself, share the burden with your partner. Together, bring the canoe over your heads, and rest the leading edges (toward the bow) of the bow and stern thwarts on your shoulders. This way, the bow paddler still leads the canoe on land as on water. Because the canoe is about level with the ground, vision is limited, but the bow paddler can still see 4 to 5 feet forward and, of course, see the path underfoot.

In any case, all lightweight gear that will not throw off the balance of the carried canoe should be tied into it: spare paddles, bailers, throw rope. Make sure they are tied securely. It's maddening to have a throw bag swinging in front of your face as you walk, and your balance can be affected.

THE GEAR. You aim to make a single trip with the packs. If possible, wear one pack using the shoulder straps just like a backpack, and balance the other one crosswise on the top of the pack on your shoulders. You can keep it in balance with one hand. Other methods, such as wearing one pack in front like a baby carrier, don't work well because you can't see your feet.

If you cannot get everything in a single trip, make a clear pile at the start of the portage, and designate one person sweep. He or she returns to pick up the remaining gear. Make your sweep the last person to go on the first trip. That way, he will know exactly what remains and how many people need to return to get it all.

THE PROCESS

Walk as a group and rest often, helping the person with the canoe get it off his shoulders and onto the ground. A gear carrier should always lead, keeping an eye on the trail and warning the canoe carrier of any surprises. For variety, you may want to switch off carrying the canoe versus the gear.

When portaging, recognize your abilities and limits. If it's just too much to carry the canoe by yourself, say so. You'll put much more of a damper on the trip if you fall and hurt yourself (you're likely to hurt yourself quite badly when the canoe lands on your head and shoulders). Be sensible: Carry the boat with another person, or carry gear that you can handle.

Missinaibi River, Ontario, Canada. Getting underway for another day of exploration on the water and the anticipation of finding an ideal riverbank campsite.

continued from page 96

posal when you get home. The campsite has a pleasing symmetry to it: the canoes stacked against each other, and the tents arrayed around the cooking area. You sit with your back to one of the canoes and watch the sky darken and listen to the water sounds on the shore. If poetry is "a momentary stay against confusion," so is this. Enjoy it, and know that you have the basic skills to renew experiences like this again and again for the rest of your life. Not a bad prospect.

ADVENTURES ON MOVING WATER

As beautiful and varied as are the experiences lakes offer, you have come to the place where the water flows downhill. You want to put your boat on that current and go where it takes you. This is a wonderful place to be, floating in a canoe amidst all that power, and once you understand a few house rules, you'll feel very much at home.

Today you are standing on a bridge, looking down at a river as it swirls beneath you, then races ahead around a bend to disappear from view. It flows through 8 miles of pretty farm country to the next bridge, and you want to run this section today to get acquainted with

moving water. Let's look at the water and share some rules that will apply on this run and on every other run on moving water. First, let's agree on some terms that are universal among canoeists who run rivers.

1. All rivers, of course, flow downhill from high country to low, so we use the terms *upstream* (above something) and *downstream* (below something) when talking about moving around obstructions such as boulders, fallen trees, or ledges.

2. To simplify left and right, we refer to *river left* and *river right*, which mean the left and right banks of the river *as you look downstream*, the way the river is flowing. This helps when

The first rule of river paddling: Stay in the center of the current. For your early outings on moving water, choose a stretch or river with plenty of current, but no white water.

discussing where to go in rapids later: River left and river right are *fixed*, you do not change your reference whether you are facing upstream or down.

In this chapter, I'll limit my descriptions to what you will need to know about rivers with a drop of 4 to 10 feet per mile, with no real rapids but plenty of current. Here are a few things you need to think about.

Water Weight

Water has weight: about 8 pounds a gallon. But even small rivers carry so many gallons of water every second that there is a more useful measure: cubic feet per second, or *cfs*, the number of cubic feet of water that flow past a point every second. This is

the measurement of river flow that you'll find in many locales by calling the water authority that regulates dams and stream flows in your area, such as the Tennessee Valley Authority in the Southeast, the Bureau of Reclamation in the West, and the Army Corps of Engineers everywhere. For most of us, however, cfs doesn't pack much of a visual wallop. A friend of mine who is an excellent instructor and capable of explaining the physics of moving water, once put it this way: An average bathtub holds 3 cubic feet of water. Visualize that! A small mountain stream, flowing at about 600 cfs, has 200 bathtubsful of water flowing by *every second*. A big river, like the Colorado through the Grand Canyon, at 24,000 cfs, has 8,000 bathtubsful of water flowing by each second. When you get to the really big tuskers like the Mississippi at 1,000,000 cfs, with a stately armada of 333,000 bathtubs sailing by each second, the power is truly astounding. But even on the little mountain stream, think of the power pushing you around.

RULES OF MOVING WATER
Respect the River's Power
How to handle all that power from a little canoe?

Respect it, and follow this simple rule: The bigger the river, the bigger the power, whether or not there are rapids. This seems painfully obvious but is ignored by canoeists who don't start paddling toward where they want to go early enough and tend to get swept into situations they meant to avoid, such as overhanging branches on the outside of a bend or a highway bridge abutment. Little streams require tighter maneuvering but don't have the same *oomph* pushing your boat against things, though even the smallest stream has sufficient power to pin your boat (and you) firmly against any solid object. Which brings us to the first rule of moving water.

Stay in the Center of the Current
The water is swift out there, yet generally free of obstructions and sudden changes in current speed. We are not talking about rapids yet, just swift water; so once you are out there, enjoy the ride. Notice that you can take all your usual lake strokes exactly as you did on the lake — no special leans. You are moving at the same speed as the water, so you don't have to worry about leaning downstream or upstream. And if you want to change direction, simply take the appropriate turning stroke to point your boat, then paddle forward and go there. Which brings us to the second rule.

Look Where You Want to Go
Look where you want to go, not at what you hope to avoid. This becomes even more important when you get to

66 I had often stood on the banks of the Concord, watching the lapse of the current, an emblem of all progress, following the same law with the system, with time, and all that is made; ...the chips and weeds, and occasional logs and stems of trees, that floated past, fulfilling their fate, were objects of singular interest to me, and at last I resolved to launch myself on its bosom, and float whither it would bear me. 99

— Thoreau,
A Week on the Concord and Merrimack Rivers

To maintain control on swift water, you must be moving faster than the current, yet that doesn't mean frantic sprinting. When you're not paddling at all, you're going at the same speed as the current; to outpace it, simply paddle steadily forward.

white water with its tighter moves and increase of seemingly confusing variables, so form good habits now. And work on developing the "wide field" of awareness that every good river paddler needs. Doing so will improve your driving in rush-hour traffic as well, because this is a principle that

TECHNIQUE TIP

BEWARE OF SHADOWS

Many river valleys are deep and narrow enough that sunlight is cut off for long stretches, even in the early afternoon. In spring and fall, when the air is still cool, that lack of warming sun can take you by surprise, making you suddenly chilly. Bring extra clothing, even on seemingly benign sunny days.

every car and motorcycle racer knows: If you look at the obstruction you are afraid of hitting, you will hit it. If you see the river pushing toward a fallen tree on the outside of a bend, fine. Note that the tree is there, then look where you want to go to avoid it.

Aim for the Inside of the Bend

When the river bends right, aim right; when it bends left, aim left. And do so early. Setting up an angle early is probably the biggest predictor of success in negotiating any stretch of swift or turbulent water. If you wait too long before setting your angle toward the inside of the bend, all that weight and speed will take you straight toward the hazard you had hoped to avoid. Besides, you want to get into the habit of surveying the scene ahead of you and setting up your angle of descent.

Setting your angle early, even in a narrow chute, allows you to paddle toward where you wish to go — the line of water that moves clearly downstream, threading between the shallows on river right and the possible hazards on river left.

Move Faster Than the Current

To be in control on swift water, you need to be moving faster than the current. (There is an important exception to this rule, but I'll deal with it when I explain back ferries in Chapter 8.)

RULES OF MOVING WATER SIMPLIFIED

⬤ The fastest water flows down the center of the river.

⬤ If the river bends, the fastest water is pushed toward the *outside* of the bend. If the river is bending right, the fastest water is pushed to the left, up against the river left bank.

⬤ When the river gets narrower, the water picks up speed.

⬤ Obstructions that block the river's flow create *eddies* downstream of them, where the water swirls in behind the obstruction.

⬤ Fast water is stable; you don't need to lean one way or the other on it as long as you are moving at the same speed as the river. Waves and other turbulence we associate with swift water can create instability for a canoeist, but speed alone does not. Water can be moving at great speed and yet be quite flat.

⬤ All instability associated with fast water occurs in zones where the current changes speed or direction: below obstructions in eddies and where fast water hits slow, piling up on itself in waves.

Moving faster than the current needn't involve frantic sprinting. When you are drifting down a river, you are going the same speed it is. All you have to do to go faster is paddle steadily forward with decisiveness, loading the paddle blade and driving the boat where you want to go.

The feeling of helplessness many paddlers experience on moving water comes from their failure to generate forward speed toward their goals. Moving water is heavy but not all that fast. Even swift-water rivers rumble along at only 4 to 6 miles an hour, a walking or jogging pace. You've got time to do what you need to do, but you have to be decisive in getting your boat moving. When you do get your boat moving, remember the final rule of swift-water tactics.

Recognizing Eddies

When crossing a current line, lean your boat in the direction of the turn.

What current line? What's that?

Don't worry, watch the river. If the fast water goes toward the outside of the bend, where does the slow water go? To the inside of the bend. How can you tell? The fast water's location is betrayed by lines of force that show most clearly at the margin of the slow water. At the zone where the two current speeds meet, you can see small whirlpools and bubble lines running lengthwise down the river. They haven't become rapids yet, but they obey the same principles rapids do. On the inside of the bend, you can see the quieter water: It is smooth and apparently darker on the surface, lacking the ripples and disturbances of the faster water.

It's at the margin of the two current speeds that you'll feel wobbly. As the bow of your canoe enters the quiet, slower water, its stern is still out in the swift current. The bow slows down, the stern swings round, and suddenly you're sitting in the quiet water, facing upstream.

The difference in current speed is most profound where an object such as a bridge piling entirely blocks the river's flow. Notice how the water swirls around below such obstructions and then flows back upstream toward the piling. This is called an *eddy*. Now look downstream with newly attuned vision; you will see eddies everywhere, some tiny with no visible obstruction creating them, others many yards wide below boulders or ledges jutting into the river.

Recognizing eddies is the single most important aspect of reading the river. Whenever you see one, you know that the water is slowing down — or even flowing upstream — and that when your boat crosses over that line between the eddy and the fast water, you must lean your boat in the direction of your turn just as you would if you were going around a corner fast on a bicycle.

That's all you need to know for now. Cogitate on these things while we set up our trip today.

SETTING UP A SHUTTLE

Setting up a shuttle is the most frequently bungled of river arrangements. Usually such miscalculations lead to great accusatory stories told in retrospect with much humor. But bungled shuttles also lead to the straining of friendships, real discomfort, and sometimes outright danger.

Rivers, with the small exceptions of the eddies within them, only flow one way. Unlike lake trips, you can't take out where you put in. You must run your shuttle first, leaving at least one vehicle down at the take-out, the bottom of the run, with food and dry clothes for all trip participants. This is important for many reasons, but primarily because you always want to have your vehicle support at the bottom — where the river is carrying you — in case you are delayed or have a mishap on the trip. Work out your shuttle details beforehand, making sure you have both a road map and river guidebook for the section of river you are running.

Ideally, you will have all cars of

A TYPICAL SHUTTLE

As I've warned, shuttles are easily muddled. If you take the time to plan yours along the lines described below in a hypothetical shuttle, it won't pose a problem. To run an 8-mile stretch of the River Spey, Sheila, Bert, Ernie, and Erica have to determine the following before running their shuttle:

How many canoes? Three: Sheila and Bert paddling a tandem, and Ernie and Erica going solo in two other canoes.

How many vehicles? Two: Sheila's Toyota wagon and Ernie's immense 4WD Detroit Bruisemaster.

Do the drivers know where the take-out is? At the put-in, Sheila and Ernie compare maps to find Speyside Bridge on Route 209. Sheila agrees to lead, and they pick a spot to meet — the gas station at the intersection of Routes 209 and 123 — if they get separated.

Can all the boats and people be taken back to pick up the top vehicle in one trip? Yes, Ernie's Bruisemaster can carry seven folks and four open canoes if need be.

RUNNING THE SHUTTLE

① Both cars, carrying all the canoeists and their gear, meet at the put-in at Lagavulin at 10:00 a.m. to unload boats and gear.

② All boaters unload the boats and put their gear in the canoe

continued on page 108

they will be paddling. Each person puts a towel and change of clothes in Ernie's car, which will be left at the take-out.

❸ The shuttle drivers, Sheila and Ernie, prepare to leave. Before they do, every member of the party goes to the boat he or she will be paddling and checks to make sure that the necessary gear is actually in the canoe. Each person also checks to see if his or her change of clothes has made it into Ernie's truck. At this point, everyone also agrees on where the keys to the take-out car will be hidden. Should anyone need emergency help, it's vital that the location of the ignition key to the take-out vehicle be known to all members of the group.

❹ The shuttle drivers proceed to the take-out at Speyside. Once there, they leave Ernie's truck, taking care to lock the vehicle and hide the keys on the truck.

❺ Sheila and Ernie return in Sheila's car to Lagavulin. They lock Sheila's vehicle up, hide the keys in the same place — under the left rear bumper — and remind the others where the keys to both vehicles are hidden.

❻ The group puts out on the river and runs down to Speyside.

❼ At Speyside, the group loads all the canoes onto Ernie's Bruise-master. They do this while still in their river clothes: Loading canoes after a trip is often a wet job. They then change into the dry clothes and pile into Ernie's car for the return to Lagavulin to pick up Sheila's vehicle.

❽ Back at the put-in, the group loads Sheila's canoe onto her car, sorts the necessary river clothes into their owner's car, and then drives off to the nearby town of Mauk Chunk for haute cuisine at Tom's Boom Chain Tavern.

all trip participants down at the take-out arranged through a commercial shuttle service or the goodwill of noncanoeist friends acting as shuttle drivers. Ideals are seldom attainable, however, so you'll find yourself running your own shuttles. Avoid howlers such as locking keys in the vehicle, losing keys on the river, or driving to the wrong take-out — all of which happen with amazing regularity. Just take your

Four tandem canoes being loaded for a run down the Chipolo River in Florida. Before setting off, each canoeist should double-check to make sure that all of his gear is in his canoe. Although you'll be eager to set out, take your time and be certain that everyone knows the location of the take-out and other details of your shuttle arrangements.

time, think things through, and make sure everyone is clear on the plan (see "A Typical Shuttle," page 107). But before you run your shuttle, all members of the paddling group should be able to put their hands on the essentials: boat, paddle, PFD, shell clothing, food, and first aid kit.

GEAR FOR MOVING WATER
Boats and Paddles
For a swift-water (but not white-water) trip, you will be able to fare just fine with nearly the same gear that you use on lakes. Standard canoes do well on swift-water streams, as do standard paddles and PFDs, but there are a few additional precautions you should take. On swift water, *always wear your PFD.* Current speed can quickly turn spills into serious situations. Wear your PFD.

Flotation for Your Canoe
While all modern canoes are designed to float even when swamped, you'll want additional flotation in the form of inflatable float bags when paddling on rivers. You don't need quite the amount for swift water that you do for white water: bow and stern float bags are sufficient (see "Securing Flotation For Your Canoe," page 112).

TECHNIQUE TIP
EXPECT SHUTTLE DELAYS...AND PLAN FOR THEM
You call your three fellow canoeists on Thursday night to confirm a time and meeting spot: 8:00 a.m. at Miz Zip's Cafe in Ponder City, about 5 miles from the put-in. Insist they come early. By the time you run the shuttle and get into your gear, it will be close to 11 a.m. It's a good idea to have a sheltered pre-trip meeting place with access to a phone. That way, if one of you is delayed, the group can be reached. Nothing is worse than hanging around at a cold put-in parking lot for hours, trying to figure out why friends are late (Are we at the wrong put-in? Did they say next Friday?) and whether to put in without them. Also, this gives you a chance to carbo-load on Miz Zip's buckwheat pancakes. Go ahead. You're going to burn off the calories.

8:30 Friday morning finds you well into the second pot of coffee when your friends arrive, giving the usual excuses. Get used to it: Paddlers are always late. That's why you demanded the early starting time. After the obligatory round of insults, you finish your breakfast and agree to drive to the put-in below the dam.

Remember: Everybody, experienced or not, swims a few times every paddling season. If your boat is without additional flotation, it will be floating at or just below the surface, heavy, difficult to stop, and begging to be pinned against a boulder or abutment and damaged. Securing additional flotation in a boat displaces water when the boat is swamped and helps it ride higher, avoiding pins and making it much easier to retrieve.

End Lines

Moving and whitewater canoes should be equipped with end lines, or painters, of 1/2-inch polypropylene rope (which floats) tied to the bow and stern decks. Each line should be about the length of the boat. Store the lines under a shock cord mounted on the bow and stern deck.

All canoes — whether a serious solo whitewater model like this one or an all-purpose tandem boat — need extra flotation when they're taken out on rivers. Inflatable float bags secured in bow and stern displace water when the boat is swamped, helping it ride higher and making it far easier to retrieve. Note also the end line and spare paddle secured under shock cords.

You will need the painter when self-rescuing with the boat.

Throw Rope

A throw rope is the one absolutely invaluable tool in river rescue, yet it is often overlooked by paddlers in their preparations for a trip. Every canoe should have a throw rope at least 60 feet long, and every canoeist should know how to use one. Knowing how to use one means being able to consistently throw the rope to and pull to shore a swimmer who is floating by 30 feet from you (see Chapter 9, page 176). The *throw bag*, which contains the

TECHNIQUE TIP

KILLING TIME PRODUCTIVELY

Shuttles by definition mean waiting — and squelching a strong desire to just leave your buddies behind, to get going down the river. But while your friends drive off to leave a car at the take-out, you can take your boats down to the water and paddle around, generally loosen up your muscles, and practice some moves. It's a great way to kill time and build skills.

A throw rope and throw bag are essential whitewater safety tools. Buy one and practice using it streamside so that you can reliably throw rope to and pull to shore a swimmer floating by you 30 feet from shore.

rope stuffed, not coiled, in it, makes such rescues easier to learn and execute; it can be thrown almost immediately from any situation. Price ranges from $30 to $75. You will want instant access to your throw rope, so clip it to a thwart or seat in your canoe with a *carabiner*.

Shell Clothing

The root of many accidents in canoeing can be traced to the fact that paddlers got tired and cold and made serious judgmental errors. Even on a simple day trip, take some of the gear that you took with you on your overnight camping adventure on the lake. The introduction of current speed makes it more likely that you will get wet, so you must have adequate clothing. Always carry shell clothing for upper and lower body: the basic "paddling jacket and pants" offered by many

SECURING FLOATATION FOR YOUR CANOE

The minimum acceptable flotation for moving water is two tapered float bags about 30 inches long that stow under the bow and stern decks of the canoe (see "Flotation for Your Canoe," page 110). They extend 16 to 18 inches into the boat from under the decks but do not come so far forward that they interfere with either paddler's knees or feet.

Float bags must be very securely strapped in; it is their nature to want to pop out. Here's

how to secure them:

● Run thin (parachute-cord type) lacing back and forth over the float bag between the gunwales. Many whitewater canoes' gunwales now come with small eyelets for this purpose. If your boat doesn't have them, drill a series of 1/8-inch holes on the inside of the gunwale (taking care not to drill through the side of the boat!). Space the holes about 6 inches apart. The lacing keeps the bags from shifting.

● Run a strap of 1-inch-wide nylon webbing over the bag. Attach one end of the strap to the grab loop that runs through the outdoor manufacturers.

LAYERING. I take a set of synthetic long underwear with me on all trips. With the revolution in the past decade of quick-drying outdoor fabrics, there are any number of affordable options in this area. Buy synthetic (polypropylene or house name, such as Capilene from Patagonia), and bring along layers appropriate to the temperatures and conditions you will encounter. The big mistake many newcomers make is judging only the air temperature, not water temperature, and neglecting to bring insulating clothing on a mild day. If you spend an hour up to your waist in 55°F water freeing a pinned canoe, you are going to be very, very cold — cold enough, per-

haps, to be unable to take care of yourself or to make prudent decisions about the rest of the trip.

Food and Water

Take both, but especially be sure to take water. Because canoeists are on — and sometimes in — the water all day, they often forget to drink enough water. Consequently they get headaches, become irritable, and are more liable to make mistakes late in the day. A bare minimum of water is one quart per person, but you should carry two.

First Aid Kit

As I've said, a first aid kit is ineffective without the knowledge to use it.

---

end of the canoe. The other attachment point must be glued to the floor of the canoe. Special nylon circles with small D-rings sewn to them can be purchased for this purpose for about $4 a piece. They come with tubes of epoxy, and it is a short job to make a permanent lashing point in your boat. These same patches can be used for securing any accessories into the canoe or providing anchor points for thigh straps, if you decide to further customize your boat.

Inflate the bags just enough that they hold their shape, but leave plenty of wrinkles in them. If you fully inflate them, they will overinflate and possibly burst as the

sun's heat expands the air inside. When storing the boat, deflate the bags and preferably remove them from the canoe.

Get basic first aid training before heading out on the river. A standard first aid kit is sold by the American Red Cross, and there are several excellent ones sold by Adventure Medical Kits (see Sources & Resources). A basic kit capable of handling the minor abrasions and injuries you are likely to see on regular trips (cuts and sunburn) costs $25 to $40; more elaborate kits for more remote situations and serious injuries go up to $150.

Other Gear

Use the same watertight gear and skills in packing that you would use on a lake outing (see Chapter 5). Be sure you have a tough outer bag with one or more layers of trash bags or zip-lock bags in which to stow your dry clothing, food, river map, and first aid kit. I always take ten large plastic trash bags. They are invaluable for many things: impromptu paddle jackets, insulating layers for an injured person, and, not least,

something in which to carry out trash you find from other thoughtless people.

Duct tape, which can be used for everything from mending float bags to lashing thwarts back together, is always worth taking along.

Finally, include a knife with a locking blade or, better yet, one of the Leatherman general-purpose tools that contain most of the tools you will need to make field repairs that Murphy's Law dictates will invariably arise.

It seems to take longer to describe all this gear than it does to throw it into your dry bags and canoe and be ready to paddle on the river. The point is to be prudently prepared, which allows you to keep the mishaps that occur on all adventures from turning into serious problems. Preparation frees you up for the joy that is yours when you swing your boat out into the current and head downstream, following a great blue heron that just lifted off from the shallows on river right.

SELF-RESCUE BASICS

We've paddled downriver for about 3 miles now, and you and the other members of the party of first-timers have been thinking that this moving-water stuff is easy. You have kept your canoes in the center of the river and, at the hint of any turn, angled them toward the inside, steering well clear of the outside of the turn, where the current has undercut the banks, causing some big sycamore trees to fall into the water and create dangerous strainers, or sweepers, against which a boat or person could be pinned. You did fine and have reveled in the sense of speed as the river carries you through the landscape. You decide that this is an elegantly lazy way of seeing pretty country.

Which is why you are not paying close attention as the river narrows, speeds up, and makes a fairly sharp bend to the left. A huge boulder sits in the water on the river right, and you are heading straight toward it. There are no rapids, but the speed of the water has increased. Your bow partner notices this speed a little late and does a hard cross draw to her left to pull the boat away from the rock. She gets her bow pulled away from it, but the boat is now almost sideways, with the stern swinging down toward the rock. You can see the rock coming at you and, determined not to look at it or hit it, do hard draws to pull your end away from it.

Surprise! No sooner do you commit to your hard draw on the upstream side of the canoe than you feel your weight shift, see the gunwale dip toward the water, and hear the squawk of your partner as she loses her balance, grabs the gunwale for support, and flips the boat on top of you.

That's how fast it happens. Are you in danger? No, not if you follow a few basic rules of self-rescue.

Rules of Self-Rescue

GET ON YOUR BACK WITH YOUR FEET DOWNSTREAM. Let the PFD float you. This way, you can look downstream over your toes, see what's coming, and, if necessary, ward it off. You want your feet visible above the water to avoid the possibility of them becoming trapped in underwater obstructions.

STAY UPSTREAM OF YOUR CANOE. You do not want to get between your boat — now full of water, weighing hundreds of pounds, and moving downhill at 5 miles per hour — and a rock or anything solid.

MAKE VOICE CONTACT WITH YOUR PARTNER. Call out to your partner to make sure she also is upstream of the boat. Both of you should swim to the same end of the boat, find the painter, and, holding onto it and not the canoe, swim into the quiet water on the inside of the turn.

You will find it surprisingly difficult to lug a swamped boat into quiet water, but help will arrive quickly: One of your partner boats will paddle up, toss you their stern painter, and help tow you over to shore. Once the water is as shallow as knee height, you can stand up, empty the boat, and, amidst general laughter, begin to dissect what went wrong.

That, in a nutshell, is a self-rescue (for more on self-rescue and assisted rescue, see Chapter 9). Once you've accomplished one, you will have learned the pathetic fallacy that precipitates so many first-timers' flips: an attempt to pull yourself *upstream*, away from an obstruction, using turning strokes.

Here's what happened: Your boat had little speed to start with and no angle as you entered the quickening current of the corner (*when in doubt, always point toward the inside of a bend!*). Your partner got the bow away from the rock using cross draws, but she did not follow the draws with forward strokes to help you pull the rest of the boat past the obstruction. No forward speed (*paddle your canoe forward toward your goal!*). You tried to reach out and pull your stern away from the rock. Did you really think you had the power to pull your stern upstream against the force of the river bearing down on the rock? This is the mistake repeated time and again by paddlers on moving water. They treat obstructions as if they were in diagrams in books like this one and seem to think that they can pull themselves upstream, away from those obstructions. Nope. Never happens. Since the boat is sitting on a sheet of current, turning strokes only change the angle of the boat. *To go somewhere, you've got to paddle there!* If you can believe in and execute this concept, your moving-water skills will increase amazingly quickly, surpassing those of paddlers who have been loafing their way down rivers for years.

LEAN TOWARD OBSTRUCTIONS

Since we are exposing the prime mistakes novices share, let's look at another. If your boat had actually hit that big boulder sideways, would you have leaned *toward* the rock (downstream) or *away* from it (upstream)? Like most folks, you probably would have leaned away from the obstruction you feared hitting, and so would have committed a cardinal sin. RULE: *Always lean toward obstructions you are about to hit.* While that may seem counterintuitive, it is essential. Leaning toward the obstruction presents the canoe's hull to the oncoming water, the water deflects off the hull, and you're given time to work your way to the side of the rock where you are more likely to bounce around and off. If you lean away from the obstruction, you are dipping your upstream gunwale under the oncoming water, allowing the river to pour its full force (remember all those bathtubs?) into your boat, sinking it against the rock

Ideal Teaching Spot

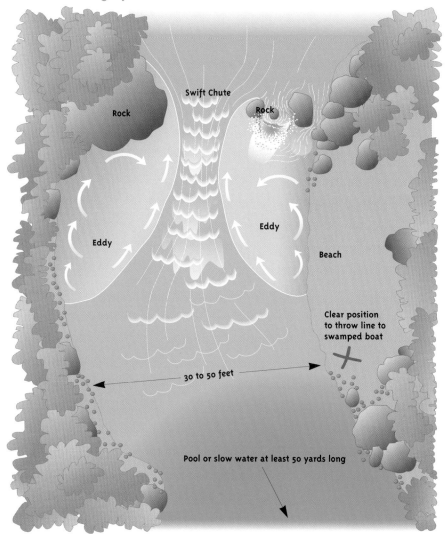

Swift Chute

Rock

Rock

Eddy

Eddy

Beach

Clear position
to throw line to
swamped boat

30 to 50 feet

Pool or slow water at least 50 yards long

Look for a stretch of river that comes as close as possible to meeting the characteristics of this ideal, safe spot. You want a swift chute — preferably with eddies to either side so that you can practice on-side and off-side eddy turns — followed by a 50-yard stretch of slow water.

and pinning it there.

Now that we are sitting downstream of our little spill spot and have processed the information gained there, let's use this area to learn some new skills. First, check the stretch of river to make sure that it is a safe place to make mistakes.

Ideal teaching areas have swift water at their upstream ends, where you can work on your skills, and then flow into a safe "run out," a pool where the water deepens and slows down and where flipped boats and swimmers can be recovered. There should be no rapids or hazards below into which swimmers or boats might be pushed. It is in areas like these where you will effectively learn your skills: not in simply running rivers.

A fully-outfitted whitewater canoeist and his craft. Note that the canoeist is wearing his helmet and PFD, that his canoe is equipped with a float bag in the bow, and that all of his gear is stowed in dry bags that are secured to the boat. He is clipping his throw bag into place just ahead of his stern paddling position where it will be easily accessible.

WHITE WATER!

You've been learning at the right pace. You are in control of your craft, and you have the good sense to listen to the counsel of the falling waters, which will give you the signals you need to make good decisions. This chapter is about how to read those signals, how to pay attention to them, and how to apply the skills you've learned to what for many canoeists is the peak experience of their sport: the controlled descent of whitewater rapids.

Before we begin with details of equipment and technique, let me point out some self-imposed limitations of this book. Skilled paddlers of open canoes have descended the most extreme stretches of white water in the world, from the gigantic waves of the Niagara gorge to incredibly steep and constricted creeks like North Carolina's Green River Narrows to 50-foot waterfalls in Tennessee. This book does not cover the skills and techniques necessary for such demanding runs. It is limited to whitewater skills just above the middle range of paddling difficulty: Class III and IV on the International Scale of River Difficulty. For most recreational canoeists, there is ample excitement and adventure in running white water up to the middle of the scale, which includes a total of six levels of difficulty. Most tandem

THE HELMET ISSUE

There is no question that helmets add to the safety of any venture where the canoe might flip and the canoeists might strike their heads against the boat or a rock. In my opinion, however — and it is one borne out by a majority of canoeists — helmets are not necessary on moving water short of white water. The flips are not especially violent, and paddlers in open canoes tend to fall out and away from the boat when it flips. On moving water — again, short of white water — there are few obstructions to strike. In such situations, I don't wear a helmet because I like canoeing for its simplicity.

Here is my compromise. I take a helmet with me on all my whitewater trips. Where the water flows deep and slow, or even deep and swift, and the rapids do not exceed Class III, I often choose not to wear my helmet. If I stop to play at a wave or a hole, I put my helmet on.

I *always* wear my helmet if I'm paddling a whitewater boat outfitted with thigh straps and foot braces and designed to be rolled. In this type of canoe, my head will indeed be underwater for seconds at a time if I flip, and I do need the added protection a helmet affords. I make my decision based on the circumstances rather than on blind adherence to a rule, and I believe you should as well. In white water, wear a helmet if the rapids are shallow and rocky or if you see that you are entering a section of rapids that is challenging to you. Especially when you are starting out, err on the side of caution; when in doubt, put your helmet on.

canoe teams find that extended stretches of Class III white water are the upper limit of enjoyable river running because, with the extra weight of a partner, open canoes tend to fill up with water in such rapids.

Running white water means getting a feel for the power of moving water, learning to anticipate where you want to go on the river, and maintaining good forward momentum so that you can deftly maneuver the boat at all times.

To be comfortable in water of greater difficulty requires paddlers to address issues beyond the scope of this book. If that aspect of open canoeing appeals to you, see the Sources & Resources section for books and videos that will prove useful.

Now for the rest of us, there are thousands of whitewater runs across North America that offer beauty, challenge, and risk enough for many lifetimes. And you don't have to continue seeking out harder and harder white water to find challenges. You can continue to refine and improve your skills for years on rapids well within your comfort range. But first,

let's look at the equipment you will need.

BASIC GEAR FOR WHITE WATER

Skill is still the most important piece of gear you can have, but in white water, you need specialized equipment: boats designed to turn on a dime and made of materials that can take a hit; personal protective gear; and gear to get you out of tight places when things go wrong.

The Canoe

When we began our sessions together on lakes, I was relaxed

This 16-foot Freedom Mad River tandem canoe is nimble in white water (note that it has some rocker), yet has the ample capacity (1,100 pounds) required for river camping trips. It is made of tough Royalex molded plastic and weighs 75 pounds.

about canoe materials and designs: Beg or borrow anything you can — aluminum, wood, fiberglass. For white water I am less easygoing. Get a boat made of plastic. By plastic, I mean a vinyl/foam/plastic laminate that originated under the brand name Royalex in the early '70s and is now the standard material for whitewater canoes. You can run white water in aluminum canoes, but they are noisy, skid to a stop on every rock you touch, and are wickedly easy to pin. Wood boats should be treated like the patricians they are and not subjected to the abuse of white water.

The premier builders of whitewater canoes in this country — Dagger, Mad River, Mohawk, Old Town, and Whitesell — all offer boats made of Royalex plastic or something like it. The chief beauty of it is its resilience. If you do wrap a Royalex canoe around a rock or an obstruction, it will rebound to its original shape after you extricate it. Extraordinary stories abound of plastic canoes dropping thousands of feet off the pontoons of bush planes on flights into Canadian wilderness rivers, cartwheeling off rocky beaches, and being used immediately by the shaken (and relieved) expedition members upon landing and inspecting the boat. Get a plastic canoe, and take the time to outfit it properly for white water.

Time to Specialize?

Every maneuver outlined in this book can be performed by either tandem or solo paddlers using the same kind of canoe. One of the great advantages of the canoe as a vessel is that a single boat can answer so many different needs and do very well in a variety of situations. Every move I describe is reasonable for novice paddlers in a general-purpose plastic canoe

between 15 and 17 feet long. It is true that a 13-foot whitewater canoe with plenty of rocker and specially rigged with thigh straps, foot pegs, and full-length airbags is a much higher performance vehicle for those desiring to run or play in hard white water. But that little canoe is a poor choice for going any distance on a lake camping trip and would be unusable if you wanted to paddle with a partner. For now, stick with general-purpose models that can handle a multi-day lake camping trip, maneuver white water up to Class III, and be paddled efficiently by a solo paddler. Once you get into the specialty boats, a delightful set of decisions awaits you, but you can develop a tremendous amount of experience and skill in a good all-round plastic canoe.

Preparing for White Water

You have shelled out good money for the extra gear to make your first whitewater experience comfortable

and safe: "How am I going to put all this stuff to use?" Well, many of the preparations and practices you began with your first trips on moving water are going to pay off now. You know you have to do the following things:

1 Get at least two other boats of paddling partners whose skills are at least the level of yours. (Three boats is the accepted minimum for safety in numbers. With tandem canoes, this means six folks; with solo canoes, three.)

2 Choose a river according to its level of difficulty. For beginners, that means Class I and II rapids maximum, unless you have an experienced leader at the club or professional level, in which case, she or he can help your group decide.

3 Arrange where to meet people and to set up the shuttles. (See Chapter 6 for details on setting up shuttles.)

Now since

Waterproof, inflatable dry bags keep gear and food safe and dry even after that moment of truth when you flip your canoe. Remember, it happens to everyone, so be prepared.

The solo cross forward stroke, with its tricky feathering recovery, is one of most difficult moves to perfect. Here a canoeist practices the stroke on a benign stretch of river. The best way to gain whitewater skills quickly is to practice moves over and over at such a safe site.

you are in the learning phase of white water, let me repeat the suggestion made in Chapter 6: The best way to develop whitewater skills quickly is to practice moves repeatedly at a safe site. Most folks learn to run rivers by running lots of rivers. Seem obvious? Yes, but the problem is this: River running allows you to get down rapids on the "tonnage and velocity" school of paddling, which relies disproportionately on speed and luck to get through rapids. Another way involves running much shorter sections of rivers and using certain rapids as practice sites to isolate and perfect moves before going on to others. "Working" rapids this way might mean that you run only a 3-mile section of river, but you play and practice so much that it takes you six hours to do so. Spending lots of time on short sections of rivers early in your paddling career means that you'll perfect skills before you embark on longer more ambitious river trips.

FIRST WHITEWATER TRIP: SHORT AND SWEET

Unless you have a designated trip leader with considerable teaching and rescue experience (for a list of where to find those, see the Sources & Resources section), you should bite off the white water you try in small, digestible chunks. Find a short run (fewer than 3 miles) with lots of Class I and a few Class II rapids in which to practice skills. Ideally, this run will be close to a road, so if you have difficulties or are really into playing at a certain spot, you can quickly get to your shuttle vehicle.

"Sounds great!" you say. "How do I find such a river?"

There are many local sources for figuring out where you are going to spend your first days on white water. Every region of the country has its standard set of beginner runs. You can find out about them from the store where you bought your gear or from the paddlers in the local club you have joined or by reading through the region's guidebook. Every paddling region in the United States has fairly extensive and detailed guidebooks that contain excellent information. You'll also find that popular beginner runs are often heavily used. While that may offend your wilderness sensibilities, it's a sure

✅

ESSENTIAL WHITEWATER GEAR

EACH PADDLER TAKES:

- PFD with rescue whistle attached. See section on signals, Chapter 9, page 169
- Paddle
- Helmet
- One set midweight poly long underwear
- One wool or poly ski hat
- Wool or synthetic fleece sweater
- Paddle pants and jacket
- Wool socks and sneakers
- Lunch and water
- Small dry bag containing spare sweater, wool socks, gloves, and ski hat
- Baseball cap and polarizing sunglasses and sunscreen

THE GROUP TAKES:

- Secured spare paddle: 1 per boat
- Throw rope or throw bag (in the lead canoe)
- Duct tape (1 roll)
- Ten plastic trash bags
- First aid kit (in the sweep, or last, canoe)
- Thermos of hot chocolate
- Dry bag with extra sweater, hat, and poly underwear

way to meet other like-minded folks and offers an additional measure of safety.

"So what does the whitewater rating system mean to me?"

All you need to know about the international rating system is that it is divided into six sections. For your first year or two of paddling, you need only be concerned with the first three, unless you drop everything else to learn this sport or invest heavily in the services of a professional guide and instructor.

There is a considerable jump up in difficulty each time you move up a grade. Furthermore, the grades do not tell you how continuous the rapids are: They only grade for the largest rapid on a given section of river. Some guidebooks adjust for this by putting a + by the grade if the rapids are long. For example, a II+ series of rapids could be quite long and complex. Though no individual move would be too difficult, a canoe taking on water would quickly get into trouble, and a flip could result in a long and unpleasant swim. Finally, as techniques and gear improve, many people tend to down-rate rapids. For novice canoeists, that can lead to serious underestimations of runs. Be cautious. When in doubt about your ability to run a rapid, carrying your boat around it is always an honorable option.

So you've made your choice. You've found your river, gathered your friends, assembled your equipment, and run the shuttle. Now as we paddle downstream, let's listen and look for the sound of our first rapids.

THE BASICS OF WHITEWATER FEATURES

You've seen the basic shape of water when it moves; now just add the admittedly distracting and sometimes downright impressive effect of air bubbles frothing up the picture. You know that the fastest water goes down the middle of the channel when the river is straight and that it pushes you to the outside of the bend when it curves. You know that slow water lags on the inside of the bend and lurks just downstream of every obstruction blocking the water's flow. All you have to add are some more details on eddies, waves, rocks, and holes. Then it's just a matter of spending the rest of your canoeing career figuring out what to do about all of them.

Eddies

By far the most important skill of the whitewater paddler is his ability to recognize eddies. Here's the simplest way to learn their basic shape: Look for swiftly flowing water along a riverbank that is from calf- to knee-deep. Walk into it and stand with your legs together, facing downstream. Now look straight down at the water swirling around your knees. That's an eddy. Notice some important things about it:

The canoe in the foreground has just crossed the eddy line and the bow paddler is taking strong forward strokes to pull the boat into the eddy. Across the chute, another pair of paddlers rests in the calm water of their eddy.

The water piling up on the backs of your legs gets deflected off at an angle. How much of an angle? About 45 degrees, but note that the strongest deflection is closest to the obstruction that forms it. This water, in fact, is some of the fastest-flowing on the river. Please note that it is shooting away from the obstruction (your legs). That's why so many canoeists miss eddies. They point at the eddy they want to catch and are

GOING SOLO

Many solo paddlers like to switch paddling sides when ferrying so that they are able to paddle on the downstream side. I do not recommend this while you are learning. It's true that it is easier to catch and control loss of ferrying angle with a stern draw rather than a pry, and being on the downstream side of the boat feels more stable when crossing the eddy line, where the current tries to push the boat out from under you. However, whenever you can, you should practice staying on one side (other than using cross strokes) to develop full competence using all the strokes in all situations. If you spend a lot of time switching sides, particularly while you are

continued on page 128

learning, your body does not get the deep awareness of what stroke to do, but rather has a frantic impulse to get on the other side where things might (or might not) be better. Don't be tempted — that's why it is important to cement these concepts in non-threatening places while you're learning.

The other solo stroke that you will find yourself doing as you practice eddy turns and peel outs on your own is the cross forward stroke. This is necessary because, particularly in today's quick-turning whitewater canoes, you find the boat pivoting too much away from your paddling side. For example, after turning into an eddy on your off-side using a crossbow sweep or draw, the boat wants to continue turning toward

that side, often to the point of going right back out of the eddy into the current. Just remember to turn the indicator thumb of your grip hand toward your head and push down with your grip hand. The boat will stop its swing to that side: The stroke will tend to hold the boat's position in the eddy.

The cross forward stroke (see page 76) is also useful to solo paddlers ferrying across the current and paddling on the upstream side of the boat. If you start to widen your angle too much, taking a cross forward stroke on the downstream side will help propel your boat across the river. The stroke is a difficult one to do repeatedly because of the dexterity required to get it out of the water, but used correctly at the proper time, it helps alleviate that helpless "spinning teacup" feeling that the novice boater often has when going it alone on white water.

surprised when the deflecting current throws their bow downstream.

2 The line between current and eddy is strongest closest to the obstruction. Forever more, I will call that line of demarcation between eddy and current the *eddy line*, and you'll know what I mean.

3 The eddy flows upstream against the obstruction and does so most

strongly closest to the obstruction.

Look at that water move back up in the pocket created just below your knees. Notice also that the farther downstream from your knees you look, the weaker the eddy becomes, until it fizzles out altogether. Your canoe needs to enter eddies right at the point below your knees where the eddy is strongest if you plan to catch and stay in them. If you set an angle but don't assertively drive the boat along it and across the eddy line, you'll be forever frustrated, nuzzling eddies with your bow, then swinging sideways and failing to stop in them.

All eddies obey the principles shown by this tiny one at your knees. Stand there for a second and get a friend into the water with you so you can see something else.

Waves

Your friend is watching you stare fixedly at the water like some obsessive Labrador retriever. Get her out here. Have her form an eddy of her own. Stand side by side, about an arm's length apart. After she's figured out eddies, look at the space of water between the two of you. See how it gets compressed into a wide V, with the tip pointing downstream? That is the mythical downstream V that canoeists always talk about but rarely see from the water level. The V is formed by fast water getting squeezed into a chute between the two of you, and that is precisely where you want to aim your canoe when negotiating rapids. A good rule to remember: Downstream-pointing Vs point to the channel, upstream-pointing Vs are eddies pointing to rocks and obstructions.

Move closer together, almost shoulder to shoulder. As the chute narrows and the water speeds up, what forms downstream of it? Waves! Without any rocks under the water creating them, a little line of waves appears. Why? Because the fast water of the chute between you is hitting slower water and piling up. Which leads us to the following conclusion: Good waves — waves that don't pose hazards — come in sets, or lines.

Those are waves you want to aim for, unless they are simply too big for

---

TECHNIQUE TIP
CARVING EDDIES

The same principle of rotation that you applied to your strokes will help you cross current lines with confident stability. On easy eddies, don't even worry about turning strokes: They are less important than sensing this concept about carving the boat into and out of the eddy using the rotation of your body. A common mistake is turning too early.

Remember, you want to drive into the quiet water. Tandem boats should begin their rotation when the bow paddler's knees cross the current line. Solo paddlers should drive into the eddy until the thwart in front of them is across the line before rotating.

Not all waves march down chutes in straight lines. In more powerful rapids like this one, water bouncing off the shore or several boulders causes reactionary waves, which can form at odd angles to the current creating a confusion of white water.

eddies. You know that fast water is being deflected off of, or squeezed between, them. Go there, pointing straight downstream. If you want to catch and stop in an eddy, you know that you must approach it at a strong angle to punch through the deflecting current that guards it. That's it. Almost all the water reading you need, right at your feet! Well, we do have a *little* more to talk about.

your canoe. But in most of the rapids you will be running in your first season or two, you will want to go where the waves are straight down the V and through the series of waves. Such a series, or line, of peaked waves marks a place where the current is constricted, faster, and probably deeper. A good place to go.

What if you don't have as clear a vantage point entering a rapid as you do looking at this little water world downstream of your legs? No problem. Looking downstream, all you have to do is search for the

Breaking Waves and Stoppers

You can come out of the water now and warm your feet up. Waves, as they get steeper, build up to a point where they start to break upstream on themselves. That break point is the lip of white water you can see at the peak of the wave. It only represents a splash and a little water in your boat as you go through or beside it. But if the wave has steepened to the point that a large amount of the top is collapsing upstream back into the trough, you have a stopper. Given enough size, this white water can actually stop a boat; or, if you go into one at an angle and unawares, it could flip your canoe. In itself, a stopper is not dangerous, but it can fill your boat up with water, making it difficult to handle and possibly leading to a flip.

REACTIONARY WAVES. Not all waves line up obediently and march down chutes in straight lines. In more powerful rapids, water bouncing off the shore or large obstructions can cause reactionary waves, which often form at odd angles to the flow of the current. Even these are not a problem if you T-bone them. By that, I mean turn the bow of your boat toward the wave so that you cross it at a right angle, making a T, rather than have it hit you from the side and roll you over.

POUROVER. We've agreed that waves come in series or obviously deflect off something. There is one more water shape to be aware — or, rather, wary — of. If you see what appears to be a big rounded wave all by itself with white water splashing up below, *avoid* it. Many river runners call this form a pourover. It is most often caused by a boulder shouldering up from deep underwater with a lot of water going over it. Pourovers are difficult to read from directly upstream, so skirt it to the side. What you will notice is that it has a very steep drop on its downstream side into a hole, which I'll describe in just a moment.

Rocks

You don't have to be afraid of rocks, but you do want to avoid them. They are clear signposts that eddies sit just downstream, waiting for you to carve gracefully into them and survey the river below. You also know that because of the deflecting currents, or pillows, piling off of the upstream side of rocks, you do not have to miss every one by a mile; the current will help push you away from them. That does not mean you can get lazy and allow your canoe to approach them sideways. You need to maintain downstream speed. Just remember what to do if you do hit one from above: lean downstream toward it. That will prevent you from flipping, filling the canoe, and possibly pinning it against the rock.

Some rocks are undercut. Their upstream side below the waterline is concave, and debris — or unwary boaters and their boats — can become lodged there. Most undercuts are immediately recognizable by the absence of a pillow of water deflecting off the upstream side. Instead, the water flows down under the rock. Often, you'll see logs and debris sticking up from the upstream face. Avoid! And don't assume that all rocks with pillows are not undercut. Let's just avoid rocks.

Holes

Holes are perhaps the most feared water feature on rivers, but they need not be. Like rocks, they give you

RESCUE PRACTICE

Just as you practiced spills and rescues on one of your early lake trips, it's an excellent idea to do so in white water. Such practice flips serve many purposes: You learn that safety systems really do work, how quickly a boat and paddler can be pulled to shore, and exactly where your balance point is by deliberately going past it.

First, check to make sure that the water is deep and the rapid does not wash out into further rapids. Then sta-

tion one of your friends at the bottom of the eddy with a rescue rope, and keep another person ready in a canoe to help tow you in if the rope should miss. Paddle out of the eddy in a standard peel out, only this time make no attempt to rotate or lean the boat in the direction of your turn as you cross the eddy line. You will find that you do not even need to lean the wrong way. Just lean in the wrong direction, and the oncoming water pushes the boat out from underneath you, flipping you upstream.

As soon as you go into the water, get into safe swimmer's position: on your back, with head up and feet downstream of you. Try to keep hold of your paddle, then stay upstream of the boat, grab its painter, and start trying to swim it to shore. When you hear the call "Rope!" be alert, looking in the direction of the call. If your companion has made a good throw, stay on your back, run the rope over your shoulder, and let your friend pull you and your boat into the eddy.

Another benefit of practicing swims is that it lessens fear of the unknown; you'll be looser and will paddle better afterward. All this assumes that the day is mild enough, the water warm enough, and you brought along adequate clothing and a towel to keep from getting chilled.

pretty clear signals of what to avoid, if you know the signals and heed them. Holes are powerful — on high-volume rivers, they have the impressive strength of collapsing ocean waves — and they deserve respect. Found downstream of obstructions, a hole is the most extreme form of a collapsed wave. The water has built into a steep enough wave to break back into and fill the trough just upstream of the wave with aerated white water, creating a depression in the river where the water flows back on itself. It circulates only once before flushing out the sides or the bottom of the trough. On a fully formed hole,

Heading over Seven Foot Falls on the Chattooga River in South Carolina. The frothy white water at its base is a hole. It is formed where the power of the water dropping over a falls creates a depression in the river where the water flows back on itself. Note that the stern paddler is maneuvering the boat by pushing off a rock.

the water is flowing upstream with considerable force. In the most powerful holes, a canoe going straight downstream can be stopped, pulled back into the pit of froth, and flipped upstream. But even in holes like these, the paddlers are usually flushed out immediately. (If your ears prick up at "usually," see Chapter 9, Whitewater Features and Safety.) Once you learn to recognize holes, you'll see that they are predictable and can be a source of play when side surfing, a technique with which you will dazzle your friends shortly.

Hydraulics

The hydraulic is one kind of hole not to play in. Hydraulics form whenever water is flowing over, rather than around, an object. A sort of vertical eddy is created, and it can easily be seen because the down-pouring water actually forms an eddy, with a line of upwelling white water called the boil line downstream of the drop creating the hydraulic. You can see the white-water surface at the boil line and race upstream into the trough at the base of the drop.

The worst hydraulics are those formed beneath sloping artificial ramps and dams. Although these often look innocuous, the symmetry of the returning waters traps boats and boaters far longer than naturally occurring holes. These are described in more detail in Chapter 9.

These are the major players in your water-reading decisions. There are endless variations, and sometimes, like English grammar, the rules get broken: A mound of water you would swear contains a pourover turns out to be a clean wave. But these are still good rules to go by as you build experience. Let's put on the river and build some experiences now.

GEAR TALK

RIGGING FOR A FLIP

Murphy's Law rules the universe. It would be foolhardy not to clip everything in so that you don't lose it in case of a swim. But don't overdo it: Many people mistakenly tie in all sorts of things — bailers, ditty bags, and so on — with nylon cord. In the event of a flip, there is a danger that you'll get tangled up in all that stuff, and even though the cord is small-diameter, it's too strong for you to break by hand.

The solution: Glue a vinyl D-ring patch (about $4) to the floor of your canoe. The same D-rings are used to attach airbags to the canoe. Clip your gear to the D-ring with carabiners or very short (less than 6 inches) lengths of line. Some people use shock-cord sections to hold bailers and spare paddles in place. Use whatever system you want, but make sure you cannot become entangled in it.

Cork Screw Rapids on the Chattooga River. This is challenging Class IV water of the sort you should avoid until you have honed your skills on less wild water. Carrying your boat around such rapids is always an honorable alternative.

BASIC WHITEWATER MANEUVERS
Eddy Turns

The eddy turn and the ferry are the foundation of all competence and control in whitewater paddling. The experts do the same basic moves we do: They just do them in extreme situations, and they always execute each stroke properly. We've paddled downriver about half a mile. You and your partner in the bow have done a fine job avoiding the rocks you have seen, she making the quick decisions about which way to go, taking the appropriate turning stroke, and then pulling you past the obstruction with forward strokes. You, in the stern, have complemented her strokes well,

helping her turn the boat, then driving it with her around obstructions. Last week's low-speed mishap has been a lesson well learned. Your confidence is growing, and you're ready for more.

Up ahead you see it: a swift chute squeezed between two large boulders on the shores of the river. The chute is 30 feet wide and drops about 2 feet into a swift race of foot-high waves that dwindle after 30 yards or so into a broad pool. The current is zipping through the chute, and the large eddies on the left and the right behind each of the boulders are strongly moving upstream. You have two choices: You can line up in the middle of the chute and enjoy the

Eddy Turn

ride down the waves and go on your way, or you can stay here for a while and work on eddy turns and ferries. Guess which one I recommend. Come on, it's a perfect teaching spot! Swift current, some tricky moves to be learned, and a safe washout if you swim.

Okay, you're ready to do an eddy turn. Let's remember the mantra that should always be in your mind: Angle! Momentum! Lean!

ANGLE. You and your partner decide to catch the eddy on the left first. She is paddling bow left. To get proper angle, you both realize that you need to get away from the eddy in order to have enough angle toward it. So you swing wide (that is, more sideways to the current) to the right side of the approach. The deflecting current off the rock on the right helps throw you toward the eddy on the left. You are both paddling steadily forward to gain greater speed than the current. She does a draw to point the bow directly at the lower edge of the rock on the left. From the shore, it looks as if you are intent on paddling directly into the rock itself. Are you mad? No, your angle is perfect.

MOMENTUM. Both of you are paddling steadily forward, still apparently bent

Remember your mantra: angle, momentum, lean. From top: the paddler has set his angle from the middle of the chute and then plants his paddle on the upstream side to perform a Duffek that will pivot the canoe around and into the eddy with little loss of forward momentum. If you do not drive the bow across the eddy line, the water's force is likely to deflect your boat back into the main current.

on ramming the rock with your bow. To keep the boat's speed up, you are paddling forward and taking forward sweeps, but you are maintaining the boat's angle by doing quick pries at the end of your strokes. Otherwise, the boat would turn too much and be pointing upstream before you gained the eddy.

LEAN. Just when it looks as if you are about to hit the rock, the deflecting current pushes your bow to the right and drops it into the heart of the eddy. Both you and your partner take one more stroke together to push the boat across the eddy line. As her knees cross the line, she rotates toward her left side and plants a solid hanging draw in the eddy. The rotation causes her to sink down onto her left knee, and the boat carves into

To give yourself enough room to gain some momentum, drop down the eddy and maneuver the boat close to the line. That allows you to re-enter the swift main current with your bow angled up into it, rather than perpendicular to it. Several powerful forward strokes propel the boat across the line, where the current then helps turn it downstream.

the eddy, continuing its turn upstream. All you have to do in the stern is lean in the direction of the turn — in this case, onto your left knee — and, when the boat has turned upstream completely, stop the turn with a forward stroke and pry. Your partner has simply rolled the hanging draw into a forward stroke,

Eddy Turn. From the shore, it appears as though the canoeist is intent on paddling directly into the rock that forms the eddy, but her angle is perfect. The current deflecting off the rock will push her bow slightly to her left, allowing her to take a few more forward strokes to drive the boat across the eddy line.

and the boat stops, nailed firmly into the heart of the eddy. It's a terrific feeling: control amidst the chaos.

Peel Outs

Now, how do you get out of here? Leaving, or peeling out of, eddies is a little more difficult because you don't have the momentum of the river helping you. The boat is bobbing up

Peel Out. The paddler has just driven his boat back into the main current, where the current's force is pushing the bow around to point down-stream. Note that the paddler is leaning to his left, in the direction of the turn.

and down and the swirling waters at the top of the eddy are slurping you up toward the rock, so you both take a few back strokes to drop down the eddy and get some room to move. You also move over toward the current so that you are about a foot away from the eddy line. This allows you to go straight up the eddy, rather than come from too deep in it and there-fore be too perpendicular to the fast current when you hit it.

Ready? Go! This is where you understand the need for downward loading and rapid acceleration: You have only 10 feet to get the boat up to speed. Your bow goes across the eddy line, but you both take one more forward stroke, propelling your partner's knees out across the line. She rotates fully to her left and plants the paddle with the full force of the downstream current flowing against it. Based on that stroke alone, the boat is pulled out into the current and turns downstream. There is nothing for you to do but lean with her and go along for the ride. Once the whole boat is out of the eddy and moving at the same speed as the current, you both dig in to pull downstream. Again, you have the exhilarating sense of having harnessed the water's power — which indeed you have. The angle, momentum, lean mantra has worked again. The two moves you have done are much harder than simply running down the rapids, but the control and confidence they give you are immeasurable. You are starting to learn the river; you can stop whenever you see an eddy. This is no small matter. Just watch the people in various types of canoes and rafts who are floating past you with no real understanding of how you stopped.

What if you want to catch an eddy on the other side? Not a problem. Set up for the same sequence of angle, momentum, and lean, and drive toward that eddy line. Your bow partner will do a cross draw to initiate the turn and to complete it, and you will tend to do stern draws and pries to hold the boat's angle. Plus you will enjoy additional stability on the turn because your on-side is the same side to which you are turning. Now, since you are able to paddle up the eddies, you can spend an hour or so at this site, really cementing the skills of eddy turns and peel outs to both sides.

SWITCH POSITIONS. You would be wise to switch positions so that you can understand the whole turn from the perspective of the other end of the boat. Changing positions will also improve your performance when you try these maneuvers in a solo canoe. There, you will notice that you must make a strong effort to power the boat forward and take correction strokes on every stroke to hold your boat on line. Also, it will be critical that you drive at least the front third of the boat into the eddy before you try to plant your duffek turning stroke. The best turning stroke in the world isn't worth much if you can't get to the eddy to place it. The stroke around which you pivot the boat must be placed solidly in the eddy.

The Ferry

An upstream ferry is a way to get your canoe from one side of a river to the other. You begin the ferry with your bow pointing directly upstream, then set an angle upstream and across while in the quiet water, keeping that angle as your boat enters the current. Since both paddlers are paddling forward, quartering into the current, the boat will make its way directly across the river at the chosen angle, with the force of the current keeping it from progressing upstream.

If you pointed your boat directly across the river rather than angling it upstream and across, the moment your bow hit the speeding current,

Solo Canoeist on Ferry. Note the sharp upstream angle of the boat as it enters the main current. The canoeist is paddling on her upstream side and has good rotation. She's performing an effective pry correction stroke to hold her upstream angle as she makes her way toward the opposite bank.

you would either flip as the boat was pushed out from under you or be swept downriver far below where you wanted to be, or both. The faster the current and the wider the river to be crossed, the more difficult the ferry. FIND THE BEST ANGLE. Swift water, not white water, is the best place to

TECHNIQUE TIP
FERRYING ESSENTIALS

● Start with the least possible angle (almost straight upstream) in the quiet water, and increase the angle as needed once the boat has entered the main current. It is easy to let the boat swing wide but much more difficult to point it back upstream against the current.

● Start as parallel to the current line as possible. If you start from deep in the quiet water, you will find that you are almost sideways when you reach the main current and will tend to be swept downstream.

● As you cross the current line into the faster water of the main channel, lean the boat slightly toward the direction you are going.

learn ferries. With no abrupt changes between fast and slow waters to grab you, all you have to do is experiment with your angles as you cross the current.

Speaking of angles, let's make sure our terms are straight. *Too little angle* means pointing straight upstream; you are paddling against the current but not going across the river. *Too much angle* means you are sideways to the current and are getting flushed downstream. The perfect ferry is a compromise between the two extremes. In tandem teams, the angle is controlled by the stern person with pries and stern draws; the bow person just chugs ahead with forward strokes to hold the position. Solo paddlers must control angle *and* paddle forward, hence the need for the effective correction strokes we practiced so much

Cross the eddy line with as little angle as possible, heading almost directly upstream. Once in the current, you can increase your sideways angle. Press down on one knee to lean the boat slightly toward the direction you are going, in this case the right knee. This will lift the upstream edge of the canoe's hull.

on the lake.

When crossing a swift eddy line the first time, do so with little angle (pointing almost straight upstream) and go out into the current with good speed. Once in the current, you can increase your sideways angle as much as you want — that's easy. Decreasing your angle so that you are pointing back upstream is harder, but perfectly possible if your correction strokes are effective. Rotate enough to the side so that your correction strokes

Time for a break. Quiet water and a broad beach are good excuses to pull up on shore to relax, snack, skip stones, and take stock of your progress.

do not create a lot of drag: They should be done pretty much in line with the hull of the boat. This is particularly true of the pry. Depending on which way you are headed, you will tend to use either the stern draw or the pry to increase or decrease your angle. In both cases, you must execute the correction stroke quickly, then return to paddling forward so that you do not wash downstream.

LEAN INTO YOUR FERRY. As you cross the current line into the faster water of the main channel, lean the boat slightly toward the direction you are going. For example, if you are facing upstream and intend to ferry across the river to your right, *lean right* as you enter the current. If ferrying across the river to your left, *lean*

to the left. NOTE: This refers to your left and right, not river left and river right. Those are constants. To lean slightly, press down on the proper knee, left or right. This will lift the upstream edge of the canoe's hull.

It's time now to go on downriver, crank turns into every eddy you see, and move back and forth across the current in ferries that are finally starting to glide. It's only a couple of miles to the take-out, but the dance is too much fun to go home early.

WHITE WATER REFINED

Another weekend is upon us. Time to go back to the river, to the place where we polished our ferries, eddy turns, and peel outs. We are not yet going out on a pure river run. There is still some gloss to put on the basics before we commit to engaging a river on its own terms. Today, we are going to learn to harmonize with water that leaps back upon itself — waves and holes.

Playing on the river will show you how much you still have to learn in terms of boat control and prevent you from making the dangerous error of wanting to run harder and harder rivers without adequate technical preparation for them. You can run a harder river every day on your home stretch: just do more difficult maneuvers in play. We are going to work on skills that you can refine for the rest of your paddling career.

BRACES

I've waited until now to teach the brace strokes: high brace and low brace. They used to be taught early in the sequence of whitewater moves, crippling generations of canoeists into leaning on their paddles for support in moving water. That's a mistake: If you are leaning on your paddle for support, you cannot use it to propel you where you want to go

This specialized canoe is known as a whitewater playboat, and is designed and rigged for serious whitewater fun. Instead of conventional seats, it features sculpted foam saddles in which to sit and thigh straps to provide greater control.

— you've given up directional control. If we're going to learn the brace, let's learn to apply it with the least possible force: no paddles slapping the water desperately; no neck tendons tight with tension. Let's use it as a gentle lever to get the canoe back under us and nothing more.

A brace is a stroke in which you use the paddle for support, rather than to move the boat anywhere. It can be wonderfully effective if you are truly about to tip over, but canoeists need to understand that real stability in the boat comes from keeping your head — literally — over a relaxed and supple center of gravity. With balance like that, the paddle is a tool for taking us places. But everyone gets out of balance sometimes, hence the brace.

The problem with teaching braces is that they are counterintuitive: Students want to push hard with the paddle against the water to brace themselves back into the canoe. Alas, such attempts always end the same way, with the student pushing down hard on the paddle, which sinks rapidly. The student then lifts his head high to get back over the boat and succeeds only in getting a gulp of air before flipping. It's an effective way to get that last gulp of air, but not very good for righting the boat. Try my way instead.

The Low Brace

The low brace is used for support when you are losing your balance *toward* your paddling side. To execute the low brace, the knuckles of your grip and shaft hands must be facing *down* toward the water so that you are placing the non-power face of the paddle as flat as possible on the water for the momentary support it offers. But even the paddle flat on the water doesn't offer much resistance. Put the paddle out on the water, and start to push down on it. It starts to sink. How does this thing work?

The low brace is a coordinated movement of the body and the paddle. As you tip toward your paddling side, the first thing into the water should be your grip hand. That's right, your grip hand, knuckles down. As soon as the grip hand enters the water, begin pulling

The low brace is used to support you when you're losing your balance toward your paddling side. It requires turning the knuckles of your grip and shaft hands toward the water so that you can place the non-power face of the blade flat on the water. By quickly levering the paddle, you get momentary support; just enough to keep the boat upright.

up on it. This allows you to maximize the amount of time the paddle blade is flat on the water. It also creates a natural levering action: As you pull up on the grip hand, you are forced to push down a bit on the shaft hand, putting a little weight on the blade and buying you the time to get back over the center of the boat. If you push down on the shaft hand first, the blade enters the water at a diving angle, which won't support you at all. As your grip hand moves up out of the water, bring it back in over the centerline of the boat. What's the rest of your body doing?

Throughout the process of the low brace, keep your head over your grip hand, eyes looking straight down on it. Keeping your eyes on your grip hand will keep your head low. Following it means that your head moves out over the water as you lose your balance, then back in over the center of the canoe. In a canoe with thigh straps, you will finish the brace by lifting the knee of the leg on your bracing side. This picks the boat up underneath you to complete the movement and bring you back to center.

I know, I know. You don't believe me. This runs so counter to what people want to do that they need to be coaxed through the process. Here's a good way to learn: Have a partner stand in waist-deep water. Put your paddle out to your side in low-brace position, and have your partner hold onto the blade. Go through the process described above, concentrating on getting your grip hand into the water first. Put as little weight as possible on the blade, but if you overcommit, your partner is supporting it to allow you to get your balance back. Repeat this exercise until you can follow the brace sequence with almost no weight at all on the blade. At this point, have your partner stand by your off-side, ready to grab the gunwales if you start to flip. Learned this way, you'll find your balance point without the anxiety of tipping over every time you err. Interestingly enough, once you find your balance point using this method, you'll discover that you rarely need to use the paddle at all for a brace: You'll simply adjust with your head and knees.

answer. If you are losing your balance away from your paddling side, simply reach out toward your paddling side as if you were going to do a draw and try to grab the water with the paddle. This is a high brace: Your knuckles will be facing up and away from the boat, and you will be pulling on the power face when you get the blade in the water. This takes less time to explain because it does not defy instinct. It does, however, take some time to develop it as your primary reaction. Usually, when novices lose their balance toward their off-side, they give up completely in that despairing gesture of grabbing the gunwales for support, an understandable but hopeless response.

REFINING FERRIES

Let's warm up with our basic ferries. Remember, the purpose is to get across the river. Canoeists repeatedly make the mistake of beginning their ferries from too deep in an eddy, under the impression that more speed will help them. Speed does help, but not if you hit the current almost sideways, causing you to be swept downstream. The trick on all ferries is to start next to the eddy line and parallel to it. Dropping downstream in the eddy to gain a couple of strokes' running start is

The High Brace

"What happens," you ask, "if you tip over toward your off-side?"

An excellent question with a simple

The high brace (right and above) can save you from a flip toward your off-side. It consists of a quick, strong draw-like move to your on-side that pulls the boat back into balance. Note the height of the hands and that the knuckles of both hands face up and away from the boat.

fine, but it is more important that you leave the eddy at a small angle with your bow pointing upstream at 11 or one o'clock.

Tandem Ferry

Remember your distinct jobs: The bow person provides the steady forward power, and the stern person controls the angle. When in doubt, keep a small angle. It is easy to increase the angle once in the current but much more difficult to lessen it, since that requires turning the boat upstream against the current.

After ferrying back and forth across the river several times to remind yourselves how this process feels, try this: Ferry out to the middle of the current. Now decrease your angle until the boat is facing directly upstream (in this case, you are doing a stern pry to lessen your angle). The pry will turn the bow of the canoe back toward your paddling side. Your bow partner has been steadily chugging ahead with forward strokes. Now nose back to the eddy you just left, ferrying in the opposite direction. The point of this exercise is to get a better feeling for precise angle control when in current.

ULTIMATE BRACE: THE OPEN CANOE ROLL

The past decade has seen open canoeists running rapids as difficult as any in the world and utilizing a roll to right themselves if they were turned over in those rapids. The results are quite impressive. The roll itself is best done in a specially outfitted solo canoe with thigh straps and with the paddler wearing a protective helmet (because the roll requires that you spend a few important seconds underwater under the canoe on a rocky river, a helmet is essential). It is not overly difficult to do, nor does it require exceptional strength, but it is beyond the scope of this book. However, learning the low brace is an important step to learning the roll, for most canoeists use the low brace as the last phase in getting their bodies back to the surface and over the center of their boats.

Although he did not originate the roll, Nolan Whitesell of Whitesell Canoes has long been an innovator in teaching the technique and has used it himself in redefining the possibilities of what open canoes can do. If learning the roll interests you, see the Sources & Resources section at the back of this book for sources of information about this and other more advanced techniques.

you angle across the river; off-side, that you are paddling on the upstream side. Most paddlers feel that paddling on the downstream side makes ferrying easier. Use easy practice spots to make off-side ferries more comfortable for yourself. Otherwise, you will develop a phobia about them.

The trick to mastering off-side ferries is simply to apply good ferry technique:

Tandem ferry on the Winooski River in northern Vermont. The bow paddler takes powerful strokes to provide steady forward momentum while the stern paddler executes a pry to control the canoe's angle.

Solo Ferry

Try this same exercise paddling alone. It will, of course, be much harder, since you will be missing your faithful bow engine. Here again, the importance of being quick and efficient with your correction J or pry at the end of every stroke is critical. For the solo paddler, ferries are always either on-side or off-side. On-side means that you are paddling on the downstream side of the canoe as

Don't start too deep in the eddy, but start low enough in the eddy and parallel to the eddy line that you enter the current with good speed and very little angle. You can increase the angle of your ferry once you are fully out on the current, but don't play with it as you cross the eddy line, or you'll be communing with the trout. And remember, once you are out on that fast water and moving the same speed as it is, go ahead and take the good clean strokes you took on the lake. If you try to take as few strokes as possible to ferry, rather than a frantic flurry of them, you'll find that you are more relaxed and the boat responds better to your demands — which is the beginning of expertise.

THE BACK FERRY
Tandem Back Ferry

What is back ferrying? Let's say you are paddling on the stern right of a tandem canoe and you are heading into a rapid that pushes hard around a corner toward the river right. The current is shoving your boat toward a strainer tree on the left bank. If you know how to back ferry, no problem. You can keep facing downstream, never losing sight of the rapid, yet correct your course. You have to do a solid draw to pull your stern toward river right, then you and your partner in the bow must start back paddling. If you keep the stern upstream and at the angle that you first set, the boat will start to glide diagonally across the river toward the right side. When you are satisfied that you are pointing where you want to go, just paddle forward again. Why didn't we learn this earlier?

Back ferrying is a useful technique, but one that has gained only regional acceptance. Canoeists taught in the northcountry canoeing style, where they are often maneuvering loaded canoes down rapids in the midst of vast wildernesses, learn it as a basic move and are consequently masterful at it. To them, back ferrying to the inside of a turn is called "setting" a corner. Canoeists of the newer whitewater tradition, taught to drive forward down rapids from eddy to eddy, are quite weak in it and therefore ignore it. Back ferrying causes more American Canoe Association Instructor candidates to fail their first skills check than any other technique. But it is great fun and adds substantially to boat control in many situations. For example, in a shallow, rocky rapid where there is not enough room in the chutes for a canoe to approach eddies at the appropriate angle, back ferrying works well, since you never have to turn the boat at a wide angle to the current at any time. Let's try it.

Paddle to the swift center of the river in a section where there are no rocks or obstructions, and point your boat straight downstream. Do the following:

❶ Stern paddler, initiate the angle. Draw your stern toward the river right shore.

❷ The bow paddler is the motor (again). Have your bow partner paddle backward strongly. You should too, when you can, but be sure that you are keeping your stern set at an angle toward the right shore.

❸ If you need to increase your angle, draw more. If you are getting too much angle and starting to go sideways, ask your partner in the bow to do a cross draw. Notice how that pulled the bow to the right and lessened the canoe's angle?

As you get closer to the right bank, try changing your stern's angle toward the left shore. You can do back sweeps, and your bow partner can help angle the stern to the left by doing another cross draw, but then it's back to chugging on the back strokes for her, while you tend to the angle in the new direction.

Next, try applying the back ferry to "set" around a corner as described in the first example. Choose only turns where the river is wide open, with swift current but no hazards. Also be sure to switch positions and try it, so you can better understand what each partner needs to do. Be sure you are comfortable back ferrying to either side.

A word of warning: Back ferrying doesn't work well when the stern paddler is much heavier than the bow paddler. The stern tends to dig in and veer off and is difficult to control. On long wilderness trips down whitewater rivers, northcountry canoeists move the loads in their canoes forward to trim the boat slightly bow heavy.

Solo Back Ferry

Without the bow paddler giving you extra back-paddling muscle, back ferrying solo requires that you have real proficiency in controlling your angle with back strokes, draws, and cross draws. You'll need them all.

Try it as you did in tandem, set-ting an angle toward river right from the center of the river in a swift but unobstructed section. You will find it is not too hard when you are paddling on the downstream side: After you have set the angle with your initial draw, you simply back paddle vigorously, and the boat scoots to the right.

Going the other way will reveal your technical shortcomings. Each stroke you take on the upstream side of the boat will make you feel somewhat shaky about leaning upstream. The stroke also tends to push the boat toward a wider angle. Don't worry, it happens to everyone. If your angle is getting too wide and out of control, reach over and do a cross bow sweep toward the bow. This should lessen your angle quickly, and you can go back to your attempts at back paddling.

Resist the temptation to switch paddling sides: You'll never get over the urge to do so if you don't work to counter it on easy water like this. You will probably come to the conclusion that the back ferry is not an ideal move for solo boaters, but keep it in mind for the future, when you are becoming so accomplished at paddling forward down the river that you are getting slightly — dare I say it? — bored on your practice runs. Then you can try maneuvering through all the rapids like this, and it will open up another level of the sport for you. Now, take this game down the river with you. We're going to look for some waves to surf.

Wave surfing, among the most thrilling of all whitewater moves. You must position your boat on the downward sloping face of a wave and keep it facing directly upstream while maintaining a delicate balance between the current pushing you downstream and the gravity of sliding down the wave face pushing you upstream.

SURFING

Nothing in river running is as much fun as playing in your boat on two of the most powerful manifestations of water's force — waves and holes. To sit on a 2-to-3-foot wave carving back and forth for as long as you want while the water rushes by underneath

A NOTE ON EQUIPMENT

My emphasis throughout the book has been on skills over equipment, but as we move into this new world of playing on white water, I must acknowledge the modern canoeing outfitting systems that have made the canoe so much more a part of the paddler. At the simplest level, I am talking about straps that run over the paddler's legs; and at the most complex (and expensive), whole seat- and foot-brace systems that make the boat respond to every movement the

canoeist makes.

Thigh straps do not tie you into the boat. They run over the tops of your thighs, holding you in place securely and allowing something wonderful. With straps, when you rotate in the direction of your turn, as I have been suggesting, you not only sink down into the turn-side knee but are able to pull up with the upstream knee. This gives you a measure of control over the edges of the boat that, once you've felt it, you'll never want to give up.

you is exhilarating. It makes you feel at home amidst all the power of the river. A bonus of this fun and excitement is that the skills you develop in play will make you a much better and safer river runner.

Wave Surfing

You have prepared for wave surfing by getting in precise control of your ferries; by being able to stop at will in the middle of ferries as you cross swift current. That's commendable, but you have been dealing only with current speed. What about when waves enter into the picture?

Let's review how waves are formed. On stretches of river where the gradient is constant, waves don't form. It's only where an increase in gradient — a drop-off below a boulder or ledge, for instance — is followed by a return to the surrounding lesser gradient that water piles up to form waves. That's because the water picks up speed as it falls down the steeper gradient, then piles up when it bumps into the slower water downstream of the drop.

Unlike ocean waves, river waves stay in place as the water flows through them. That means that you can count on the wave staying the same height and behaving the same way. (This is not true on some big-water rivers, where waves build and collapse in heights up to 20 feet, but you're not getting on those anytime soon.) When you surf a river wave, you are doing a ferry and sliding onto the upstream face of a wave with your bow pointing upstream into the trough. You are sliding down the angled face of the wave while the water races by underneath you. The gravity that pulls you down the wave is countered by the speed of the water going under you in the opposite direction, so you sit in place — as long as you remain straight upstream. Once you get too much sideways angle, you're not sliding down that wave as fast, and the force of the water flowing downstream wins out, throwing you to the side and off the wave. That's where all your ferry practice will pay off, as you finely adjust your angle with precise correction strokes.

Picking a Surfing Wave

We want to find a play site that is not upstream of any hazards and has a good washout area in which to perform rescues, since there will inevitably be spills while learning to surf waves. What are we looking for in a wave? The ideal beginner surfing wave has these qualities:

❶ It should be from 6 inches to a foot high.

❷ It should be at a chute bordered by eddies so that if you miss the wave, you can regain the eddy and paddle up to try again without exhausting yourself.

❸ The wave must have a long enough upstream face to accommodate your canoe. That means that the face must be at least 4 to 5 feet long, or there will not be enough room for the boat

to slide down.
⑥ The wave must be steep enough for you to slide down. Look for a little white water breaking back upstream at the very crest — a small hem of white water. This means that the wave is steep enough for the water to build up and fall back

To surf on a wave, you must keep your boat aiming directly upstream. Once you get too much sideways angle, you're not sliding down the wave as fast, and the force of the water flowing downstream wins out, throwing you to the side and off the wave.

upstream toward the trough and therefore has the angle you need. If a lot of white water is falling back and filling the trough, the wave is probably too steep and does not have a face long enough to fit your canoe.
⑤ The wave needs to be wide enough to afford room for you to cut back and forth: at least two canoe widths, or about 5 to 6 feet. If it is too narrow and peaked, it will not be tolerant of your early correctional mistakes, and you'll get frustrated trying to surf it.

This is not the only kind of surfable wave, but these qualities make it a good bet for beginners.

Tandem Surfing

You have found your wave, and your bow partner is eager. As usual, you

are paddling stern right. You are sitting in an eddy on the river left side, facing upstream, as if you were going to ferry across. Before you begin, notice one thing that is very important about the wave: Its high point is in the middle of the current, but it slopes down to merge with the eddy. If you look carefully at a wave, you will see that it has shoulders at river left and river right that join it to the flatter, slower water of the eddies on either side. It is much easier to get on the wave if you position your bow partner so that she is kneeling on the upstream face of the wave and if you get onto that face at the shoulder — the slight depression that marks the transition from the eddy to the wave. If you make the mistake of trying to get on the face of the wave from below, you are fighting a double battle: trying to go up against the current and paddling uphill over the wave itself. Visualize the bow person kneeling on the wave, and put her there. Her job is to paddle forward upstream to give the boat initial momentum to get on the wave; yours is to paddle forward and adjust the angle.

You'll probably do several swift ferries across the river before you begin to figure it out, but these are necessary. Notice how fast the wave seemed to throw you across the river? That's because you were momentarily sliding down the face of it. The next time you go out on the wave, try doing a little pry to straighten the boat upstream as you feel the bow drop down into the trough. For a thrilling moment, the boat will actually stabilize, and you'll be surfing.

In about a second, you'll lose the angle and head back to shore. But

---

TECHNIQUE TIP

TROUBLESHOOTING THE TANDEM SURF

You get on the wave, but the bow buries into the oncoming water from upstream, and you lose your angle.

Your bow paddler is probably paddling forward when the canoe is already on the wave and driving the bow down into the trough, a common mistake.

Every time you do a pry to correct the angle, the boat seems to get dragged downstream and off the wave.

You are not doing an effective pry. Either you are moving your shaft hand away from the boat, which means you are doing a back sweep that acts as a brake, or you are not rolling your wrists back enough (indicator thumb up), and your pry is not on edge like the tiller of a sailboat but, rather, flat in the water and acting as a brake.

You and your partner are exhausted.

You've been paddling so hard forward to catch the wave, that you haven't realized when you are off it. Remember, when you are surfing, you should feel yourself being held on the wave. Your bow will be pointing down into the trough. If you see your bow level or pointing slightly up in the air, it means you are not on the upstream face of the wave but teetering on the crest or back of it, tiring yourself needlessly. Simply drop off the back, and ferry back to the eddy to rest and learn from others' efforts, then try it again.

you've felt it. Now the trick is to go out there and sustain that sensation. You can sustain it only by making small and constant correction strokes: a pry if you need the boat to straighten toward your paddling side, and a stern draw if you need to straighten away from your paddling side. It's going to take some fiddling, but when you get it right, you'll be able to sit there, your partner holding her paddle in the air and you taking small corrections to keep the boat pointing straight upstream. Because it takes a while to master surfing, the excitement of accomplishment is heightened. Remember, when learning to surf, trade positions occasionally. Your understanding of the needs of each end of the boat will make you a better canoeist.

Solo Surfing

You seem to have this tandem surfing wired: you can catch the little wave at will now, and you have enough control even to allow your angle to widen and then cut back across the wave while remaining on it. You want to try it on your own.

At first, you are going to miss the extra power of your tandem partner. You'll adjust, but as in everything else you do solo, you need to be especially sharp on your correction strokes. All the principles of tandem surfing apply, but here, there are some specific things to remember.

❶ You might initially have trouble staying on the wave. That is because you don't have the weight (or the power) of your bow partner sliding down the upstream face. When looking for surfing waves on the river, soloists generally need a slightly steeper wave than tandem boaters. Drive your bow a little deeper into the trough than you did in tandem. You want your knees to be on the upstream face of the wave, not behind it.

❷ Leave the eddy with very little angle. It's easier for you to correct once on the wave.

❸ Whereas in tandem boating, you might occasionally take a pure power forward stroke, you will almost never do so paddling solo. Every forward stroke *must be followed by some quick form of correction*, or your boat will veer off the wave time and again until you slump, enraged and exhausted, in the eddy. This is worth citing, because I see so many enthusiastic solo students missing waves as they simply paddle harder.

These exercises will keep you busy for quite some time. There are more advanced techniques to be applied, such as back surfing on waves, but the detailed description of how to do all that would be overwhelming for a beginner or novice and is beyond the scope of this book.

As your confidence grows, and you see how you can control the canoe's movement from side to side on waves of increasing size, you'll start to work out some tricks of your own, and to seek additional chal-

For some whitewater canoeists, it isn't enough to run rivers, camping along the way. It isn't even enough to find good waves and holes to play in. These paddlers seek competition on white water. This tandem team participates in a whitewater race on the Salmon River in New York State.

lenges, such as back surfing on the waves and even, in time, learning to play in holes. But that's for future trips: All your playing today has been teaching you what you need to know about the rhythms of the river and your place amidst them.

WHITEWATER
FEATURES
AND SAFETY

As a veteran canoe instructor, I've heard dozens of variations on the story of "The Trip That Changed My Mind." Told with good-natured, self-deprecating humor, they recount near misses and disasters, prime reasons for many of our participants seeking out a course of instruction: They wanted to avoid disasters like that again. Most of these stories go something like this:

"Well, it had been raining for about three days before it cleared up. Little Pine Creek was way up and out of its banks — just tearing along. My buddy and I thought it looked like a lot of fun — there weren't any rapids to speak of, but the current was tearing through the trees, flat and fast. It was a beautiful April day, so we went around and borrowed a couple of canoes and some life jackets. By the time we got all the gear rounded up, it was getting toward four o'clock, but we figured the water was going so fast that the run wouldn't take long, so we took off. Around the first bend, Gary's boat went right into a log jam, and I saw him go under. I was trying to stop getting swept into the thing myself and grabbed a branch, and WHUP! I went into the water. It took the breath right out of me, it was so cold..."

You get the idea: The two boaters swim to opposite banks, can't find each other, and wander around in the gathering dusk as they become increasingly hypothermic and worried that the other has drowned. This scenario has been played out repeatedly. Sometimes the stories are funny, sometimes they aren't. All share an admission of ignorance and a lack of preparation on the part of the teller and underline what we need to look for in planning a river trip: first and always, the willingness to consider the consequences of our decisions.

You need information before you can make those decisions on your own. This chapter contains that information. In it, you will learn what to look for and how to handle the most common hazards that you are likely to confront on rivers appropriate for your level of experience and skill. That means swift rivers with little or no white water to Class III white water.

WIDE FIELD OF VISION

Maintaining a wide field of vision means that you look at each event you anticipate with an eye toward its possible consequences. Eventually, everything on a safe trip comes back to this, from getting your cars and canoes to the river to deciding whether to run or portage around the rapids you encounter. It also means honestly answering some seemingly simple, obvious questions. If you can answer "yes" with cautious confidence to the following questions before a trip — and at any point on the trip — then you're on the right track; your adventures should be pleasantly memorable. The "you" addressed in all the questions applies to *everyone* in your group.

DO YOU KNOW THE RIVER YOU ARE RUNNING? The best idea is to have an experienced paddling partner on the trip who has run the river before. The best place to find such a valuable person is a local or regional canoe club. Check the Sources & Resources section for a directory of local clubs through the American Canoe Association (ACA). This way, even if you can't get that experienced person on the trip, you'll be able to talk to her on the phone. Canoeists like nothing better than talking to people about rivers they have run.

The next best source, and one you should obtain in any event, is a guidebook to rivers in your chosen area. Whitewater guides are available for practically every region in the United States, and they all provide invaluable information about difficulties of runs; lengths of runs; locations of put-ins and take-outs; dams and other features; remoteness; and safe water levels.

It's not enough to know about the river and its technical difficulty. You need to have accurate maps for getting to and from the put-in and take-out points. Every car carrying canoes to the river needs to have a road map or atlas.

DO YOU HAVE ALL THE GEAR YOU NEED TO RUN IT? On a standard river

Scouting a rapid on the Missinaibi River, Ontario, Canada. Before running a river for the first time, consult guidebooks that detail the white water and its difficulty. Better yet, bring along a paddler who knows the river to serve as a guide. Even then, it's often smart to make time ashore to size up rapids before running them.

run, you will take roughly the same gear listed in Chapter 6. Points to remember at the put-in: Make everyone wear the essential gear they plan to have on the river or put it in the canoe they will be paddling. Prior to driving off on the shuttle, have everyone, including yourself, put

A spill on Corkscrew Falls about midway down the Five Falls Section of the Chattooga River, along the Georgia-South Carolina border. This Class IV rapid — with equally difficult rapids upstream and downstream — is challenging even to experienced canoeists. While the River Difficulty Scale is useful, it can be misleading, particularly for beginners. Always gather as much firsthand information about a river as possible before running it.

their hands on all the gear they are taking. This method almost never fails. In my experience, the person who complains the most about being treated like an infant is the person who has forgotten something essential. MAKE SURE EVERYONE MEETS A MINIMUM LEVEL OF COMPETENCE. What if not everyone is appropriately prepared and/or experienced? What if Bill's friend Bob shows up unannounced at the put-in ready to go but without sufficient flotation in his boat and without any previous paddling experience with anyone on your trip? Most folks don't feel they have the authority to tell someone they can't go on the river with their group, and unpleasant, sometimes tragic, trips

result. Better to be forthright and explain that you're willing to take the trip with only the group already there, and tell Bob that you are not comfortable adding more unknowns to a river you don't know well. Invite him on future practice trips elsewhere, but don't buckle under and let him come! Take the long view: Think how you'll feel if his presence causes an accident for himself or someone else in your group.
DO YOU KNOW WHAT DEMANDS ON YOUR SKILLS THE TRIP WILL MAKE? The International Scale of River Difficulty (see page 161) describes individual rapids, so sections of rivers are often rated in guidebooks by their toughest rapids. In many books, that

does not tell you if the Class III section is a single large drop into a pool or a 2-mile-long gorge of continuous Class III water. Hence, the need to get as much specific information

about the run as you can.

Be aware that rivers in certain areas, such as the Rocky Mountain

text continued on page 164

THE INTERNATIONAL SCALE OF RIVER DIFFICULTY

Class ratings of a given river's challenge have been codified by the American Whitewater Affiliation, an organization that promotes whitewater adventuring in all appropriate crafts.

This is the American version of a rating system used to compare river difficulty throughout the world. This system is not exact; rivers do not always fit easily into one category, and regional or individual interpretations may cause misunderstandings. It is no substitute for a guidebook or accurate firsthand descriptions of a run.

Paddlers attempting difficult runs in an unfamiliar area should act cautiously until they get a feel for the way the scale is interpreted locally. River difficulty may change each year due to fluctuations in water level, downed trees, geological disturbances, or bad weather. Stay alert for unexpected problems.

As river difficulty increases, the danger to swimming paddlers

becomes more severe. As rapids become longer and more continuous, the challenge increases. There is a difference between running an occasional Class IV rapid and dealing with an entire river of this category. Allow an extra margin of safety between skills and river ratings when the water is cold or if the river itself is remote and inaccessible.

CLASS I: Easy. Fast moving water with riffles and small waves. Few obstructions, all obvious and easily missed with little training. Risk to swimmers is slight; self-rescue is easy.

CLASS II: Novice. Straightforward rapids with wide, clear channels which are evident without scouting. Occasional maneuvering may be required, but rocks and medium-sized waves are easily missed by trained paddlers. Swimmers are seldom injured and group assistance, while helpful, is seldom needed.

CLASS III: Intermediate. Rapids with moderate, irregular waves

continued on page 162

CLASS I

CLASS II

CLASS III

RIVER DIFFICULTY
continued from page 161

which may be difficult to avoid and which can swamp an open canoe. Complex maneuvers in fast current and good boat control in tight passages or around ledges are often required; large waves or strainers may be present but are easily avoided. Strong eddies and powerful current effects can be found, particularly on large-volume rivers. Scouting is advisable for inexperienced parties. Injuries while swimming are rare; self-rescue is usually easy but group assistance may be required to avoid long swims.

CLASS IV: Advanced. Intense, powerful but predictable rapids requiring precise boat handling in turbulent water. Depending on the character of the river, it may feature large, unavoidable waves and holes or constricted passages demanding fast maneuvers under pressure. A fast, reliable eddy turn may be needed to initiate maneuvers, scout rapids, or rest. Rapids may require "must" moves above dangerous hazards. Scouting is necessary the first time down. Risk of injury to swimmers is moderate to high, and water conditions may make self-rescue difficult. Group assistance for rescue is often essential but

CLASS IV

CLASS V

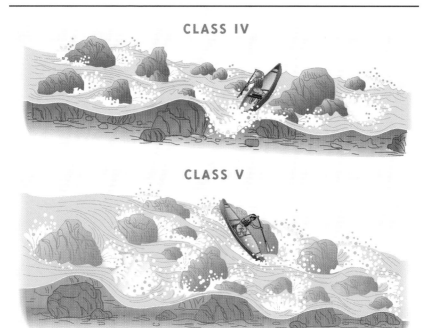

requires practiced skills. A strong eskimo roll is highly recommended.

CLASS V: Expert. Extremely long, obstructed, or very violent rapids which expose a paddler to above-average endangerment. Drops may contain large, unavoidable waves and holes or steep, congested chutes with complex, demanding routes. Rapids may continue for long distances between pools, demanding a high level of fitness. What eddies exist may be small, turbulent, or difficult to reach. At the high end of the scale, several of these factors may be combined. Scouting is mandatory but often difficult. Swims are dangerous, and rescue is difficult even for experts. A very reliable eskimo roll, proper equipment, extensive experience, and practiced rescue skills are essential for survival.

CLASS VI: Extreme. One grade more difficult than Class V. These runs often exemplify the extremes of difficulty, unpredictability and danger. The consequences of errors are very severe and rescue may be impossible. For teams of experts only, at favorable water levels, after close personal inspection and taking all precautions. This class does not represent drops thought to be unrunnable, but may include rapids which are only occasionally run.

continued from page 161

West, are generally rated for kayaks and tend to underrate rapids from a canoeist's point of view. From a kayaker's perspective, a mile-long section of swift water and 3-foot waves without any obstructions is almost unrated, while a tandem open canoe team might have difficulty getting through without swamping. If the guidebook is not abundantly clear in describing the rapids, play it safe and overrate them slightly.

DO YOU KNOW WHAT TO DO AND WHERE TO GO IF THINGS GO WRONG? This is the question that canoeists most often fail to answer. To do so, you must have good maps (topographic ones if the river is remote from roads) to maintain a sense of where you are in relation to roads, bridges, and towns as you run the river. Canoeists are apt to think that the only way out of a river is down it to the planned take-out, but in most places in the East, even a seemingly remote river will curve near a road somewhere. If there is a need to walk out, whether due to accident, injury, or approaching darkness, knowing how to get to a road or house quickly can avert a more serious emergency.

In addition to knowing your location, you need a first aid kit and the skills to use it. For basic first aid and CPR, the American Red Cross chapter nearest you is a good place to start. If you want more wilderness-oriented training, the two best-known names in the field that teach excellent courses are SOLO, of North Conway, New Hampshire, and Wilderness Medical Associates of Bryant Pond, Maine (see Sources & Resources for details).

SAFETY SKILLS AND PRACTICES
Minimum Number In a Group

Three should be the minimum number of canoes in a group. One is unwise for obvious reasons, but in a rescue situation, two is not much better. Rescues on swift water tend to be difficult. Freeing a pinned canoe usually requires the power of at least three people, often supplemented with mechanical advantage systems. Even on a narrow river, rescues often require more than 100 feet of rope. In a minimum group size of three solo canoes, you have the option in case of injury of one person staying with the injured person and one person going for help. With three tandem canoes (six paddlers) or two solo canoes and a tandem canoe (four paddlers), you have a more comfortable margin for error.

Read Rapids From the Bottom

When you first encounter a rapid, your eye tends to be drawn to the most spectacular whitewater feature — the *biggest* drop or deepest hole. In fact, the first place you should look is below the rapid; into what conditions and hazards does the

BEFORE
RUNNING A RAPID

Ask yourself the following questions:

➊ *What moves are required of me?*
As you look at the rapid, define as precisely as you can the specific moves you will need to execute to have a successful run. Does it require that you cut across current in a ferry to avoid swamping in waves on the approach? Is there an eddy that must be caught to put you on the proper side of the river above a critical chute? Be specific, not: "Oh, if we stay straight and keep our speed left, we'll be OK."

➋ *Can I do those moves?*
This is candid self-assessment. You are not asking yourself if you want to do the moves required by the rapid, you are taking mental note of your abilities. If the rapid requires ferrying across a big wave from river left to river right, and you have trouble with that kind of move — say, only a little better than 50 percent success — then, no, you're not ready to run that rapid. Not in real control, at any rate.

➌ *What are the consequences if I fail to do those moves?*
Look at the whole rapid, top to bottom, itemizing each move you

know is required. Are the difficult moves high up in the rapid, meaning that you and your canoe would be in the water for the length of the rapid if you capsized? Or are the difficulties low in the rapid, just above a large recovery pool? What kind of obstructions exist in and below the rapid? Are there any abrupt ledges over which a swimmer might go, undercut rocks that might catch a boat or person? Are there hazards such as a strainer tree in the bend below the rapid, toward which boats and swimmers would be pushed if rescue ropes failed to catch them? These are the questions you must ask as you look at the rapid.

➍ *Am I willing to accept those consequences?*
This last question is critical. If you do see a potential hazard in a rapid but decide that there is little risk of making a mistake that would make you encounter that hazard, you must still ask yourself, "Am I willing to accept the penalty that hazard might hand me, whether it be a pinned canoe, a long swim on a cold day, or worse?"

For most of us, this is not a hard question if there is a clearly dangerous hazard in a rapid — an

continued on page 166

BEFORE RUNNING A RAPID
continued from page 165

undercut rock into which the full force of the river flows at the bottom of a long and tricky Class III run. That's an easy call: Most of us aren't willing to risk our lives running any rapid. The harder calls come with more variables to consider, where an error you make in the rapid isn't likely to have fatal consequences but could set in motion a chain of events with an unpleasant conclusion. You must ask yourself questions like: If we pin a canoe here and can't get it unstuck, how are we going to get everyone to the take-out, since there is no road nearby? What time of day is it? Is everyone in the party doing well physically and mentally? Is Tom tired out after his three swims earlier? Your acceptance of consequences must extend to questions about the day.

If you can't answer all those questions with a positive response, you should carry your boats around the rapid or line them down the side, if possible. Will you make mistakes assessing

these risks? Of course, but if you err on the side of caution, you will be able to come back again with better information and more skill. White water is unforgiving of error: When things go wrong, they can go really wrong. Be cautious, but don't be paralyzed by caution. For example, if the rapid consists of an impressively steep chute into a 5-foot stopper wave above a pool of deep water, you might not be able to guarantee you can make that move. But the day and water are warm, the recovery pool is large, and you and your companions are all adequately dressed. Sure! Go for it!

The point of my insisting on this evaluation process is to instill in novice canoeists an insistence on asking the "What if?" questions for every turn and rapid on the river. The actual running through of this mental checklist takes only a few seconds on most rapids, and in time, it will become an automatic process. Remember, we aren't trying to eliminate risks — they are part of the beauty of the sport — but we are trying to learn how to intelligently assess them.

rapid run? This way, you can work your way back up to the rapid's entrance, connecting the clean lines and chutes with the confidence that

they go where you want. This method works whether you are standing on shore looking at a major falls or twisting to look over your shoulder from an eddy in the middle of a long Class II rock garden.

Lead and Sweep Positions

On all trips, designate a lead (first) and a sweep (last) canoe. These are not honorary titles — they are positions with real responsibility. The canoeist in the lead boat usually knows the river better than does anyone in the group and is a solid enough boater to be able to offer safety in all the rapids. This does not mean that the lead canoeist is an infallible expert who never swims, but that she or he is the most knowledgeable person in the party about the particular river to be run.

Three is the safe minimum number of canoes on a river-running expedition, and the roles of each boat and its team of paddlers must be clear, with lead (first) and sweep (last) positions adhered to. Note the distance between these two boats; generous yet within eye contact. Note also the nicely synchronized strokes of the lead tandem team as it crosses a deep pool.

The sweep boater is often just as strong and knowledgeable as the leader. The sweep boat should carry rescue and first aid gear so that if an incident occurs, necessary material will be coming down to the accident rather than receding downstream and away from easy access. In groups of boaters of roughly equal ability, lead and sweep positions may change many times, but always with a formal passing of responsibilities: "Will you

STOP! STOP! HELP! EMERGENCY! HELP! EMERGENCY!

ALL CLEAR: PROCEED DOWN THE CENTER ALL CLEAR: PROCEED DOWN THIS WAY

UNIVERSAL RIVER SIGNALS

STOP: Potential hazard ahead; wait for "all clear" signal before proceeding, or scout ahead. Form a horizontal bar with your outstretched arms. Those seeing the signal should pass it back to others in the party.

HELP/EMERGENCY: Assist the signaler as quickly as possible. Give three long blasts on a police whistle while waving a paddle, helmet or life vest over your head. If a whistle is not available, use the visual signal alone.

A whistle is best carried on a lanyard attached to your life vest.

ALL CLEAR: Come ahead (in the absence of other directions, proceed down the center). Form a vertical bar with your paddle or one arm held high above your head. Paddle blade should be turned flat for maximum visibility. To signal direction or a preferred course through a rapid around obstruction, lower the previously vertical "all clear" by 45 degrees toward a side of the river with the preferred route. Never point toward the obstacle you wish to avoid.

lead this section? I don't remember it well. I'll take the first aid kit and cover sweep."

The sweep boat need not always be last. In certain rapids, you might want both the strong boats low in the

Having a closer look. Three paddlers take some time to debate the best way to run a tricky rapid. Such scouting sometimes makes sense, especially when a good vantage like this one can be gained by coming ashore.

rapid to provide safety backup, so your lead and sweep might run early and help guide other boats down to them.

River Signals

The American Whitewater Affiliation (AWA) river signals have been universally adopted by river runners across the United States. Be familiar with them (see "Universal River Signals," page 168).

One river signal often neglected is the whistle: Three sharp blasts mean *Hey! Trouble over here!* If you have the ability to purse your lips and give a piercing whistle, bless you. If not, do what I do, and attach a small plastic rescue whistle to the zipper of your PFD.

One other signal that you should share with your partners: *Always point toward where you want them to go.* Generally, people try to go where you point, so if you are halfway down a rapid and pointing vigorously toward a big mound of water, that's where your following boaters will go — even if that means you've sent them into the heart of a hole you were trying to warn them away from. Be sure to point where you want them to go!

SCOUTING RAPIDS

There is a large eddy on river right just above the rapid, and you signal to your friends in the two other canoes — Rachel and Claudine in a tandem boat, followed by Gary in a

Eddy Hopping

a mound of water, below which you can see white water spraying up. Hmm, some kind of pillow or hole? It looks easy to avoid: That eddy on the left halfway down the rapid is big enough for ten canoes.

You go through all this as you look down at the rapid and decide to "eddy hop."

Eddy hopping is a fun way to scout a river *without* getting out on shore every time you're uncertain about the best course to take. It consists of the lead paddler hopping from one eddy to the next one downstream and then signaling his comrades upstream as to how to proceed. When the eddies are large enough, two or three boats can then regroup before the leader peels out and makes his way to the next eddy.

Eddy Hopping

If you stopped and got out on shore every time you were a little uncertain about where to go, it would take forever to run the shortest stretch of river. To save time, and as a pleasurable end in itself, you should eddy hop with your friends. When you eddy hop, you keep moving downstream, going from eddy to eddy and being sure that the canoes above you are able to stop in small eddies of their own. When you have seen a good route to the next

solo — to meet you there. From this vantage, you can look down the rapid and get a better idea of its challenges. You can see the rapid is a long Class II. It looks like fun. There is a long recovery pool below the rapid, which consists of about a hundred yards of small waves. The river is still bending to the left, so the fastest water is pushing out toward the river right. About midway down the line of waves on the right side of the rapid, there is

There are times, as here, when pushing off a ledge is a perfectly acceptable way to negotiate a rapid. Many canoeists make use of this maneuver when running this Class IV water at Seven Foot Falls, on the Chattooga River; this tandem boat successfully ran the falls. Notice the extraordinary degree of rotation the bow paddler has managed.

eddy, you signal to the boat upstream of yours to come to the eddy you are leaving, then peel out. In this way, two or even three boats can be in motion, weaving their way downstream with a clear and immediate goal. Picking up from where we left off with the three canoes above the rapid, eddy hopping goes something like this:

You go first to the large eddy below a shelf midway down on the left. Rachel and Claudine in the tandem canoe will join you there. You will then peel out and go to the bottom of the rapid. Only after your successful run and signal, will Gary, the solo canoeist, come down to the

first eddy, where the tandem canoe is waiting. After Gary successfully catches that eddy, the tandem boat peels out and paddles to the bottom of the rapid to join you. Gary then paddles to the bottom. You review signals to make sure everyone is on the same wavelength.

Then you peel out of the eddy and enter the rapid, driving decisively toward the big eddy on river left. Ten minutes later, you all are talking to each other, floating as a group in the pool at the base of the rapid, holding on to each other's gunwales. The first rapid went like a charm. From the big eddy partway down, you could clearly see that there was no rapid immediately below the recovery pool, and you could also get a better view of what was indeed a big hole hidden by the mound of water on river right. But there was little danger of going into the hole, since you ran the rapid with a driving angle left toward the eddy midway. The tandem boat caught the eddy, you peeled out and paddled to the pool at the bottom. The upright paddle signal was sent up the river to Gary in the sweep solo boat, and the whole process was repeated until your trio of boats sat in the pool together.

At any time, the procession can stop: The lead canoe simply signals up from the lowest eddy to wait. Although it is an effective way to move downriver, you must always leave yourself an out. Be sure that you can get to shore if you need to. Never use the technique to paddle around blind corners, since it's possible to catch the last eddy in the middle of the river above a bad rapid. Don't do that to yourself and friends. When you cannot see to the bottom of a rapid, either because it drops out of sight or is hidden by a tight bend in the river, get out and scout.

Whether scouting from a canoe or the shore, the same four questions should always run through your mind:

What moves are required of me?

Can I do those moves?

What are the consequences if I fail to do those moves?

Am I willing to accept those consequences?

RESCUES

Gary is in the water!

The next rapid hasn't gone quite so smoothly. A little unsure of paddling solo in rapids, Gary tips over while leaving an eddy. You give three long blasts on your whistle to alert the tandem canoeists and look downstream over your shoulder.

Not too bad: You are in an area of swift current and waves on a slight bend to the left. Below the bend, the river spreads out into a slow section. No hazards can you see. When you look back upstream, you can see that Gary is doing well. He has the painter of his boat and is back stroking hard to make it to the shallows on the inside of the turn. Rachel and Claudine swing down to him, give him their stern painter, and start pulling him faster to shore. When they have reached the shallows, Rachel stows her paddle and hops out of the canoe to hold everything in place. Gary stands up, gasping for breath from the cold water. You have collected his paddle, which floated down to you, and ferry over to shore to join them. The whole swim took about two minutes and 50 yards of river distance.

When you bring the paddle back to Gary, you make sure that he is OK, then insist that he get his paddle jacket off to wring out his insulating clothing. This he does. After putting back on the nylon pile sweater from which he has shaken the water, Gary does some jumping jacks to crank up some body heat and pronounces himself ready to go.

Always look downstream *first* to check what hazards the swimmer might be heading toward. This allows you to make some quick decisions about whether you will make your rescue from river right or river left, and whether the situation is serious enough to forget rescuing the boat and concentrate on the swimmer instead. Gary's case was not that serious; the river downstream of the spill was not challenging.

Rope rescue in progress, Jawbone Rapid, Chattooga River along the Georgia-South Carolina line. This Class IV water is two rapids downstream from Corkscrew Falls (see page 160), and is quickly followed by yet another rapid in the Five Falls Section of the river. A series of rapids tests the skill and endurance of the paddlers, leading to spills like this one. The recovery pool before the next rapid is short, making a successful rope rescue critically important; more than one paddler to wipe out on this rapid has drowned in the rapid just downstream.

Self-Rescue

Rescuing yourself by swimming alone or with the boat is the simplest and most effective way to get out of the drink, back to shore, and back into your boat. In rivers, the safe way to swim is to stay on your back, with feet downstream and toes of shoes visible above the water. In this position, you almost back ferry toward the

Safe Swimmer's Position: On your back, head held up, feet pointing downstream and kept close to the water's surface. This posture gives you a clear view of oncoming rocks, holes, or sweepers; prevents your feet from becoming trapped between rocks; and allows you to use your feet and legs to push off of rocks or ledges. But it is not the only safe position (see following page).

feet. And, if you're still holding the paddle (which can impede effective swimming), you can throw it to the shore or eddy to which you are heading.

This "safe swimmer's position" is necessary in most swift-water swims to avoid the danger of foot entrapment, but it should not be followed to the exclusion of common sense. If you are bouncing along on your butt in 6 inches of water, by all means stand up! If it looks

nearest shore or eddy, kicking vigorously and paddling with both hands. Why not do the crawl? Because on your back, with feet near the surface and pointing downstream, you'll avoid having your feet trapped between rocks, you have a good downstream view, and can ward off rocks and other hazards with your

as if you are not making sufficient progress toward a safe spot while swimming on your back, turn over on your stomach and do a racing crawl toward safety. If it appears that you are about to swim over a steep ledge, ball up (to prevent your extended legs from being driven down deep below the drop into a possible foot entrapment). If it looks as if you are being swept into a strainer (see page 180), flip onto your stomach, swim toward it, and try to climb up on it as high as possible. Most of the time, however, the safe swimmer's position is the way to swim in white water.

If you are swimming and still have contact with your canoe, do the following:

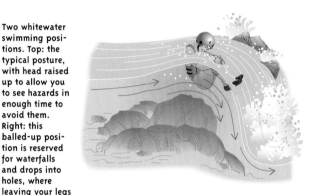

Two whitewater swimming positions. Top: the typical posture, with head raised up to allow you to see hazards in enough time to avoid them. Right: this balled-up position is reserved for waterfalls and drops into holes, where leaving your legs out-stretched can make them vulnerable to breaks or strains as you hit the bottom of the hole.

❶ Be sure to get or stay on the upstream side of the canoe. You don't want to get between its swamped weight and a rock.

❷ Grab the painter. The best way to store the painters is under shock cords on the bow and stern decks. You can reach them easily there and pull them out. Swimming upstream of the canoe at the end of the painter allows you to control the boat while staying well clear of it.

❸ Roll the canoe upright if you can. When you are at the end of the boat getting the painter, if you are in deep enough water and have the time, roll the canoe upright by pulling or pushing on the gunwales near your end of the boat. This does not empty the canoe of all water, but if you have a boat with airbags, it will float much higher and be easier to pull to shore.

❹ Be prepared to get rid of the canoe. Even the strongest swimmer cannot tow a swamped boat to shore quickly. If you see that the swamped canoe is pulling you into another unknown rapid or toward a hazard, release the boat and swim to safety. Too many tragedies have resulted from

✓

THE ROPE RESCUE CHECKLIST

Here, in a nutshell, are the steps in a rope rescue:

1. Yell "Rope" to catch the swimmer's attention.
2. Throw to the swimmer when he is still slightly upstream of you. This allows you to start reeling him in without the direct force of the river pulling against him. In fact, the river is helping you swing him to shore.
3. If you can, walk downstream and inland as you pull the swimmer to shore, just like an angler playing a trout on a light line. This way, there is never too great a force on either the swimmer or the thrower.
4. Reel him in. Always pull hand over hand on the rope, and keep your hands out of any wraps or loops in which you might get caught.

canoeists heroically staying with their boats. You can always retrieve it later or buy another one. Let the boat go.

Towed Rescue
This is an assisted rescue, similar to Gary's, above. A swimmer holds on to

the painter or grab loop of a rescuer's canoe and is towed to safety. This is very tiring for even the strongest paddler, because the drag of a person immersed in swift water is extraordinary. It is best done by a tandem canoe, since soloists of intermediate ability have trouble keeping the canoe straight against the strong ruddering drag effect of a swimmer hanging on to the stern.

When performing a towed rescue, set an upstream ferry angle and back down to the swimmer. Once the person has your loop or painter, ferry at the widest angle possible toward a safe spot. You need a wide (sideways) angle because the swimmer's drag acts as a sea anchor, swinging the canoe's stern downstream. If in a solo canoe, paddle on the outside (that is, the side of the canoe toward the river as you are ferrying to shore) using wide forward sweep strokes to keep your angle wide.

Rope Rescue
Around the bend, the river drops out of sight again. You all catch a big eddy above the rapid and look downstream. Sure enough, there is a pool at the bottom, but the river below it looks as if it is heading into another rapid. It's hard to tell from your canoe. A lot of white water and spray are obvious on the river right as well as a nasty-looking pointed rock sticking up out of the water about 3 feet. Plenty of water piles into it.

Hard to read the signals. Better get out and scout this one.

Having taken some time on shore to thoroughly scout the tricky rapid, you have run down the first chute, past the pointed rock and into an eddy. You ferry over, walk down the river left shore with your throw bag (and the one you borrowed from Gary's boat — nice to have a backup in case you miss your first throw) and set up on the shore midway down the pool. You hold the bag up in the air as a signal to Rachel and Claudine, and they respond with vertically raised paddles, then paddle into the rapid.

They hit it perfectly, entering the first chute with left angle and driving the boat forward. Their angle and speed carry them easily to the left of the pointed rock, and with additional forward strokes, they drive across the eddy line, where Claudine in the bow plants a hanging draw, swinging the canoe smartly around.

It is not Gary's day. Paddling on the right, he has not followed his forward stroke with a sufficient correction stroke, so the boat swings sharply to the left — almost sideways. To correct, Gary resorts to a back sweep, which straightens him as he enters the first chute but also kills his speed. No angle left, little speed forward. His bow is now aiming to the right of the pointed rock; Gary knows he is in trouble. Scrambling now, he takes two hard forward strokes, but then negates them with equally hard back sweeps. The canoe strikes the

pillow of water off the rock just behind Gary. He leans to the left (slightly upstream) to pull away from the rock, sinks the left gunwale into the oncoming water, and flips. You get ready for a rope throw.

Gary surfaces beside his boat midway down the chute. He immediately gets his feet up in the safe swimmer's position and reaches under the boat to grab a painter. His paddle is floating downstream of him. He is still 30 feet upstream of you and about 30 feet out in the current. You yell "Rope!," wait for his eyes to fix on you, and then throw the bag out to him when he is still about 10 feet upstream of you. A good throw: The bag sails over him, dropping the rope on his chest. He clutches it with his free hand, and you begin backing away from the water and moving slightly downstream, playing Gary like a trout until you have him sitting in the shallows at the bottom of the eddy, gasping for breath. Rachel and Claudine have ferried out, picked up the floating paddle, and returned to shore. One minute. A small problem has remained small.

As thrower, you needed to station yourself a good 30 to 50 feet downstream of where you expected a flip to be likely — a big wave or tricky ledge. Remember, you are trying to throw to swimmers *after* they have surfaced by the canoe. Choose a spot that is not dangerous to you. A flat spot by the shoreline just above a big eddy into which to pull a swimmer is

ideal. Standing atop a boulder off of which you might be pulled is not.

Be sure that *before* the need arises, every member of your party knows how to receive a thrown rope: Stay on your back in the safe swimmer's position, and let the rope run over your shoulder so that as you are pulled to shore, the water will break around your head and allow you to breathe.

ASSESSING RIVER HAZARDS

The river is narrowing and gaining some speed. Wide rapids are getting squeezed into narrower, longer lines of waves, which you run as canoeists should, just beside the peaks so that you get the good ride without taking on water. Up ahead, the river turns farther left and drops out of sight. Bigger waves are kicking up, and the sound of the water is a louder and deeper tone than what you have experienced before. You feel the excitement and slight apprehension of all explorers: What lies ahead, and how will we run this rapid?

Waves and Currents

Here lies the heart of your river-running tactics. The driest route through rapids is to drive forcefully from eddy to eddy. A canoeist coming down a tough rapid and catching five or six

eddies isn't necessarily showing off. It just might be the best way to get through a long rapid without filling up with water. On the other hand, it's great fun to run down a long line of waves; just be prepared to take on more water, particularly in tandem boats. The best place to hit a line of waves is just to the side of the peaks. That way you get a good bouncy ride without all the water breaking into the bow.

Whenever a crossing changes in current direction or speed, lean in the direction of your turn. For example, if you are driving out of a fast line of waves from river left into slower water on river right inside of a bend, rotate toward your right as you enter the slower water.

Rocks

We know we want to miss rocks, and we know that the water deflects off them, pushing us to the side if we get too close. Still, it's possible to hit them. It can happen to the best of river runners. When you do hit a rock, be sure you lean into it (or onto it), draping yourself over it and presenting the hull of the canoe to the oncoming water. Otherwise, if you enact the understandable but unfortunate error of leaning away, the incoming waters will fill your canoe and pin it firmly against the rock, from which it is holy hell to get unstuck.

Undercut Rocks

Undercut rocks are, in effect, open

Up ahead bigger waves are kicking up, and the sound of the water is a louder and deeper tone than what you have experienced before. You feel the excitement and apprehension of all explorers: What lies ahead, and how will we run this rapid?

flows — are one of the most serious hazards in any swift-water situation, particularly for swimmers. If you are in swift water heading toward a strainer and see no way of getting around it, flip from the safe swimmer's

If you cannot avoid swimming into a strainer, flip onto your stomach from the safe swimmer's position and do the crawl. As you approach the strainer, quickly pull yourself up onto it to avoid being dragged down beneath it, where your arms and legs could become snared in the branches. Strainers are among the most dangerous features on moving water.

mouths facing upstream just below the waterline. Water flowing against an undercut rock is deflected down and underneath it, often without leaving the telltale mark of solid rocks: the pillow of water that deflects off the upstream in a break of white foam. The danger of under-cuts is that debris is often lodged under them that could snag a swimmer, or the swimmer could wash under the rock itself and become trapped. Because the rock is not deflecting water off its upstream face, it will not tend to deflect your canoe as you approach it, increasing the risk of becoming pinned or pulled beneath the rock and below the water's surface. The lesson: Take even greater pains to avoid rocks that do not display a pillow of water.

Strainers

Strainers — fallen trees forming large sieves through which current

position, get on your stomach, and swim toward the strainer. This way, when you hit the thing, you'll have your hands and head up to climb up onto it quickly and strongly before you get sucked down under it. If you do get stuck, at least your head is up out of the water, where you have more time for rescuers to get to you. Clearly, however, the best thing is to avoid situations where you risk swimming into a strainer.

Stoppers, Holes, and Hydraulics

Holes are those places in the river where the water has poured back on itself to fill the trough created by an obstruction under the water. Holes are intimidating for many paddlers, just like moguls — bumps on steep runs — are for many downhill skiers. They feel that they are going to be jostled and thrown around by forces beyond their control. Well, there is

Hole   # Hydraulic

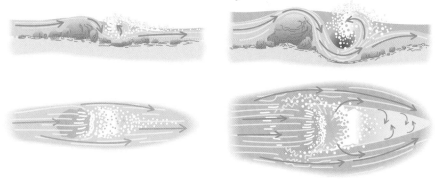

Left: True eddies do not form below holes. The river bottom downstream from a rock that forms a hole is relatively shallow, so that while a wave does collapse upstream into the hole, plenty of water flows through the hole, making it quite harmless. Right: Hydraulics are more powerful, severe holes where there is a more extreme drop-off in the river bottom and/or there is a greater volume of faster-moving water. Eddies do form below them. At a hydraulic, there's enough drop below a boulder or ledge so that the surface waves not only fall upstream to fill the depression, but strong recirculating currents run upstream, sometimes creating long eddies.

some basis for that concern. Holes are places of powerful conflicted energy on the river. But there is much joy to be had amidst that energy, if you know what to look for and how to choose the right line around it.

For our purposes, holes can be divided into three broad categories: stoppers, holes, and hydraulics. To some degree, the names are regional or national (if a canoeist from Great Britain calls something a stopper, he might mean a worse hazard than I do), but these distinctions are pretty widely shared by open canoeists in the United States. The need for distinctions isn't just semantic: It's useful to know that you can play in some holes but never in a hydraulic. Be aware that all these features exist on all rivers. You needn't live in fear

of them; just be aware of their differences and how to recognize them. The other issue is size. Even the grabbiest hydraulic isn't of concern to you until it gets big enough to affect a canoe or a swimmer. STOPPERS are waves that have built up so steeply that a great deal of the wave is collapsing back into the trough of water upstream of it. That collapsing water carries a lot of weight — it can fill up your boat or flip you if you get sideways — but it will not hold you there. Too much water is flowing downstream, and there is no eddy created below it. HOLES are stoppers that have collapsed and completely filled the trough upstream because the obstruction under the water is nearer the surface, causing a more abrupt drop with an equally abrupt backwash.

Some holes can be huge indeed, but they will not keep you underwater for long if you are swimming: you might get circulated once in the backwash collapsing into the trough, but so much water is flowing through the hole and below it that you'll soon be washed downstream and back to the surface. In the right sizes and shapes, holes are where canoeists can play. There is not a true eddy below holes: The water will have slowed down, but it will still be moving downstream. This is a useful distinction between holes and hydraulics.

HYDRAULICS are holes with the most powerful recirculating force. The obstruction creating a hydraulic is close enough to the water's surface that an eddy is formed; the current for some distance downstream moves back upstream to the face of the obstruction. Hydraulics can form below ledges or isolated rocks over which the water pours (called a pourover by many paddlers) and, in the worst case, below man-made dams. The longer the eddy, the more dangerous the hydraulic. Some low head dams that look innocuous have recirculating hydraulics where the water returns to the drop from 15 feet downstream. For our purposes, any time the returning water in a hydraulic eddy is coming in from more than 3 feet, stay away.

The shape of the hole is an important consideration: If the corners at the edge of the hole turn downstream, then it will be easier for your boat to exit, since the water will tend to push you out of the hole once you get to the edge. If the corners turn upstream at the edges, the hole will tend to form a bowl from which it is harder to escape, since the water funnels you back to the center of the hole. Some people call these "smiling" or "frowning" holes, as they would appear if you looked straight down on them from above. That image has never been memorable for me, because we never see holes from directly above, but I pass it on in case it works for you.

S O U R C E S &
R E S O U R C E S

We hope you are now eager to hit some water, and raring to start a new obsession. If, however, you need to read more, join a club, or browse a magazine, we've set out plenty of information with addresses and phone numbers below to "wet" your appetite. We start with the major national paddling organizations and groups concerned with related topics.

ORGANIZATIONS

These leading organizations provide a wealth of information for the novice canoeist.

AMERICAN CANOE ASSOCIATION (ACA)

7432 Alban Station Road
Suite B-226
Springfield, VA 22150
703-451-0141
Website: http://www.aca-paddler.org/

National governing body for canoe and kayak activity. Thirteen regional and 250 local affiliated groups. Sponsors races and classes and provides extensive information as well as publications. Publishes *Paddler* magazine and *American Canoeist* newsletter.

AMERICAN WHITEWATER AFFILIATION (AWA)

P.O. Box 85
Phoenicia, NY 12464
914-688-5569
Website: http://www.awa.org/
Promotes whitewater safety, technique, equipment, and river access programs. Also publishes *American Whitewater*.

NATIONAL ORGANIZATION FOR RIVER SPORTS (NORS)

212 W. Cheyenne Mountain Boulevard
Colorado Springs, CO 80906

719-579-8754
Promotes all whitewater sports, conservation and lobbying before government agencies. Membership includes the quarterly journal, *Currents*.

UNITED STATES CANOE ASSOCIATION (USCA)

c/o Jim Mack
606 Ross Street
Middletown, OH 45044
513-422-3739
For individuals interested in canoeing and kayaking. The USCA's Five-Star Program — Competition-Cruising-Conservation-Camping-Camaraderie — highlights its concerns.

AMERICA OUTDOORS (AO)

(formerly Eastern Prof. Outfitters Assoc. and Western River Guides Assoc.)
P.O. Box 1348
Knoxville, TN 37901

615-524-4814
For professional recreation service outfitters. Good source for outfitters and buying information.

AMERICAN RIVERS
801 Pennsylvania Avenue, SE,
Suite 400
Washington, D.C. 20003
202-547-6900
A public interest organization working for river protection. Several publications.

EASTERN PROFESSIONAL FRIENDS OF THE RIVER (FOR)
909 12th Street, No. 207
Sacramento, CA 95814
916-442-3155
Individuals and environmental groups united to preserve the great waters. Wide-ranging activities.

NATIONAL ASSOCIATION OF CANOE LIVERIES AND OUTFITTERS (NACLO)
US 27 & Hornbeck Road
Box 248
Butler, KY 41006
606-472-2205
Website: http://world.std.com/~reichert/naclo.html
This organization's website has a fabulous list of members — renters and outfitters — by state.

SCHOOLS
If these leading schools don't fit your needs, check the back pages of paddling magazines for more complete listings.

BILL DVORAK'S KAYAK AND RAFTING EXPEDITIONS
17921 US Highway 285
Nathrop, CO 81236
719-539-6851
Website: http://www.vtinet.com/dvorak/

BOULDER OUTDOOR CENTER
2510 N. 47th Street
Boulder, CO 80301
800-364-9376
Website:
http://www.boc123.com/

MADAWASKA KANU CENTRE, INC.
Box 635, Barry's Bay
Ontario, Canada K0J 1B0
613-756-3620
(winter) 613-594-5268
Website: http://fox.nstn.ca/~owlmkc/

NANTAHALA OUTDOOR CENTER
13077 Highway, 19 West
Bryson City, NC 28713-9114
704-488-6737
Website: http://www.nocweb.com/default.htm

OUTDOOR CENTRE OF NEW ENGLAND
10 Pleasant Street
Millers Falls, MA 01349
413-659-3020

RIVERSPORT SCHOOL OF PADDLING
213 Yough Street
Confluence, PA 15424
814-395-5744

W.I.L.D. W.A.T.E.R.S. OUTDOOR CENTER
P.O. Box 197
Route 28 at the Glen
Warrensburg, NY 12885
800-867-2335
Website: http://www.webtreks.com/wildwaters/wildwtr.html

ZOAR OUTDOORS PADDLING SCHOOL
Mohawk Trail, P.O. Box 245
Charlemont, MA 01339
800-532-7483
Website: http://www.deepriver.com/adven/htm/149.htm

TOUR ORGANIZERS & GUIDES
There are hundreds of liveries, guides and outfitters across the country. We have included a sampling of reputable ones serving famous canoeing regions such as New England, the Everglades, the Boundary Waters, the Southern Appalachians, the canyons of the Rocky Mountain West, and the Pacific.

NORTHEAST
ADIRONDACK CANOES AND KAYAKS
93 Old Piercefield Road
Tupper Lake, NY 12986
800-499-2174

ALLAGASH WILDERNESS OUTFITTERS
36 Minuteman Drive
Millinocket, ME 04462
207-695-2821

CAPE COD COASTAL CANOEING
36 Spectacle Pond Drive
East Falmouth, MA 02536
508-564-4051
E-mail: cccanoe@capecod.net
Website: http://www.capecod.net/canoe/

SACO BOUND/ NORTHERN WATERS
Box 119
Center Conway, NH 03813
800-677-7238

MIDDLE ATLANTIC STATES
KITTATINNY CANOES
HC 67, Box 300
Dingman's Ferry, PA 18328
800-FLOAT-KC
Website: http://www.microserve.net/~magicusa/floatkc.html

POCOMOKE RIVER CANOE
312 N. Washington Street
Snow Hill, MD 21863
410-632-3971

SOUTHEAST
APPALACHIAN OUTFITTERS
P.O. Box 793
Dahlonega, GA 30533
706-864-7117

BUFFALO OUTDOOR CENTER
P.O. Box 1
Ponca, AR 72670
501-861-5514

CANOE KENTUCKY
7323 Peaks Mill Road
Frankfort, KY 40601
800-K-CANOE-1

FRONT ROYAL CANOE CO.
P.O. Box 473, Route 340 South
Front Royal, VA 22630
703-635-5440

NO. AMERICAN CANOE TOURS
P.O. Box 5038
Everglades City, FL 33929
813-695-4666

OUTDOOR ADVENTURES
6110-7 Powers Avenue
Jacksonville, FL 32217
904-739-1960

MIDWEST
BEAR TRACK OUTFITTING CO.
Box 937
Grand Marais, MN 55604
218-387-1162

**GUNFLINT NORTHWOODS
OUTFITTERS**
750 Gunflint Trail
Grand Marais, MN 55604
218-388-2294

PIRAGIS NORTHWOODS CO.
105P N. Central Avenue
Ely, MN 55731
800-223-6565

**ROCKY MTS. AND
SOUTHWEST DESERT
ADVENTURE DISCOVERY
TOURS**
403 W. Birch
Flagstaff, AZ 86001
602-774-1926

CANYONS, INC.
P.O. Box 823-R
McCall, ID 83638
208-634-4303

**MOKI MAC RIVER
EXPEDITIONS**
P.O. Box 21242
Salt Lake City, UT 84121
800-284-7281

PACIFIC
**CANOE AND KAYAK
OUTFITTING**
3003 Highway 669
P.O. Box 699
Willow Creek, CA 95573
916-629-3516

WANTU CANOE
P.O. Box 474
Chico, CA 95927
916-891-1424

WY'EAST EXPEDITIONS
6700 Cooper Spur Road
Mt. Hood, OR 97041
503-352-6457

CANADA AND ALASKA
ALASKA TRAVEL ADVENTURES
9085 Glacier Highway
Suite 301
Juneau, AK 99801
907-789-0052

ALGONQUIN OUTFITTERS
RR1
Dwight, Ontario
P0A 1H0 Canada
705-635-2243

BATHHURST ARCTIC SERVICES
Box 820 (P)
Yellowknife, NWT
X1A 2N6 Canada
403-873-2595

**BEAVERSTONE GUIDED
CANOE TRIPS**
800 Lasalle Boulevard, Suite
197
Sudbury, Ontario
P3A 4V4 Canada
705-566-8975

NAHANNI RIVER ADVENTURES
P.O. Box 4869
Whitehorse, Yukon
Y1A 4N6 Canada
403-668-3180

MAGAZINES, CD-ROMS & ONLINE SERVICES
The canoe and whitewater magazines are chock full of techniques, recommendations, and advertisements for outfitters, organizations and trips.

Canoe & Kayak
Canoe America Associates
Box 3146
Kirkland, WA 98083
206-827-6363

Paddler
4061 Oceanside Boulevard,
Suite M
Oceanside, CA 92056
619-633-2293
Formerly *River Runner*, covers whitewater canoeing, rafting and kayaking.

Wooden Canoe
P.O. Box 255
Paul Smiths, NY 12970
Fax: 518-327-3632
E-mail:
quenelj@paulsmiths.edu

CD-ROMS
Try these newest of the multimedia products available for your home use.

Adventure Paddle Sports CD,
Rocky Raccoon Software,
$39.95.

Maniac Sports, covers many of the wilder versions, including whitewater kayaking.

Paddle Sports, covers all aspects of paddling from equipment to rescue. $39.95.

THE INTERNET
Canoeing on the Net? Even a novice can paddle those turbulent waters. Remember that web addresses change frequently, or simply disappear, so all information provided below can only be guaranteed at the time of publication.

Let http://trailside.com be your up-to-date source of outdoor recreaction information on the internet. Daily updates, user feedback, active message boards and hot links to the best websites offer broad and in-depth information for the adventurous. A great place to "put in."

Besides our own Website and addresses provided in other sections, here are some internet search paths related to canoeing.

http://www.yahoo.com/Business and Economy/Companies/ Outdoors/Expeditions Tours/ Canoeing Kayaking and Rafting/

An oddity, perhaps, if anything is on the Web: *Wooden Canoe Journal*, the bi-monthly journal of the Wooden Canoe Heritage Association; http://www.wcha.org/wcj/ index.html. It also maintains a directory of builders and suppliers of wooden canoes: http://www.wcha.org/builders.html

and Whitewater Paddling:

Send mail with the word *subscribe* in the text body to: white-water-request@gynko.cir.upenn.edu

Subscribe to the whitewater@ peak.org list by sending mail to: majordomo@peak.org. Type "subscribe white-water your-email-address."

Although originally a white-water forum, the usegroup rec.boats.paddle has more and more information and discussion about canoeing and sea kayaking.

For those of you considering subscribing to a commercial on-line provider, *America Online's* outdoor recreation and travel services offer information on and listings of outfitters, organizations, destinations and gear. It also has active message boards, chats and hosted events with outdoor experts. Belonging to AOL is a good way to access other groups on the internet. To subscribe, call 1-800-827-6364. The software will be provided to you free.

BOOKS
If you like to read or feel better easing slowly into this new ven-

ture, here are some suggestions.

CANOEING, IN GENERAL
An Adirondack Passage: The Cruise of the Canoe Sairy Gamp, Christine Jerome. 1994. $20.00. HarperCollins.

The Complete Wilderness Paddler, James W. Davidson and John Rugge. 1983. $13.00. Random House.

Path of the Paddle: An Illustrated Guide to the Art of Canoeing, Bill Mason. 1995. $19.95. NorthWord Press.

Roughing It Elegantly: A Practical Guide to Canoe Camping, Patricia J. Bell. 1994. $12.00. Adventure Publications.

Song of the Paddle: An Illustrated Guide to Wilderness Camping, Bill Mason. 1988. $19.95. NorthWord Press.

The Survival of the Bark Canoe, John McPhee. 1982. $9.00 Farrar, Straus & Giroux.

Water's Edge: Women Who Push the Limits in Rowing, Kayaking & Canoeing, Linda Lewis. 1992. $14.95. Seal Press-Feminist.

SAFETY AND RESCUE
How to Survive on Land & Sea, Frank C. Craighead, Jr. & John J. Craighead. 4th ed. 1984. $17.95. Naval Institute Press. A comprehensive manual of survival techniques, equipment and strategies for a broad spectrum of emergency situations.

River Rescue, Les Bechdel & Slim Ray. 1989. Paper. $12.95. How to avoid river accidents and how to handle them. Appalachian Mountain Club.

Whitewater Rescue Manual: New Techniques for Canoers, Kayakers & Rafters, Charles Walbridge and Wayne A. Sundmacher. 1995.

$15.95. International Marine.

RELATED SUBJECTS
Building Boats
Boatbuilder's Manual, Charles Walbridge. 1987. $9.95. Menasha Ridge Press.

Knots
The Ashley Book of Knots, Clifford W. Ashley 1993. $50.00. Doubleday & Co.

Knots for Paddlers, Charles Walbridge. 1994. $4.95. Menasha Ridge.

DESTINATION GUIDES
There are excellent navigation guides for almost all of the states, in addition to the more general guides listed below.

The Whitewater Sourcebook, Richard Penny. 1990. $19.95. Menasha Ridge Press. This large manual provides detailed information on hundreds of rivers in 34 states, as well as sources for maps, lists of organizations, schools, events, and a priceless list of whitewater guidebooks for each state.

AMC River Guides and Quiet Water Guides. $11.95-$14.95. Appalachian Mountain Club Books.

Appalachian Whitewater, Vol. 1: The Southern Mountains, Bob A. Sehlinger. 1986. $14.95. Menasha Ridge.

Appalachian Whitewater, Vol. II: The Central Mountains, Ed Grove, Bill Kirby and Charles Walbridge. 1987. $14.95. Menasha Ridge.

Paddle America: A Guide to Trips and Outfitters in All 50 States, Nick Shears. 1993. $12.95. Starfish Press.

Western Whitewater from the Rockies to the Pacific: A River

Guide for Raft, Kayak, & Canoe, Jim Cassady, Bill Cross, Fryar Calhoun. 1994. $34.95. North Fork Press.

Whitewater Quietwater, Bob Palzer & Jody Palzer. 1983 $12.95. Menasha Ridge Press. Guides to 750 miles of rivers in the Great Lakes region.

VIDEOS

Our own Trailside® series of videos which aired on PBS are some of the greatest inspirations we can offer to the novice canoeist. Available direct at 1-800-TRAILSIDE (1-800-872-4574)

Solo Canoeing in the Everglades. Watch out for alligators as you learn a new style of "water-dancing," paddle solo canoes through Everglades National Park, Florida, and camp out on a Chickee. 45 minutes. $19.98.

Whitewater Canoeing Expedition in Ontario. Adventure starts at Road's End in far northern Ontario and heads into trackless bush on the Missinaibi River. 45 minutes. $19.98.

Whitewater Canoeing on the Chattooga River. Go for "the big ride" on the boisterous Chattooga River along the Georgia/South Carolina border. 45 minutes. $19.98.

Paddling and Poling in Louisiana Bayou Country. Paddle, pole and camp on the banks of the Atchatalaya Basin, "the swamp of swamps in the state that's mostly swamp." Learn the secrets of cooking Cajun style while keeping a safe distance from the gators. 45 minutes. $19.98.

Flat Water Canoeing the Missouri River, Montana. Lewis and Clark paddled this section of the Big Muddy in 1805. Nearly 200

years later, Trailside is right on their trail. 45 minutes. $19.98.

OTHER INSTRUCTIONAL VIDEOS

To order, try the mail-order sources listed in the next section.

Introduction to Canoeing - 1990. 35 minutes. $12.95.

Complete Guide to Canoe Trips and Camping. A guide to canoeing in many wild, remote and unchanged lands. 1991. 45 minutes. $12.95.

Heads Up! River Rescue for River Runners. Produced in association with the U.S. Coast Guard and the American Canoe Association. $40.00.

How to Canoe. Basic paddle strokes and river reading. $21.95.

Paddle to Perfection. Book and video with basic instruction. 55 minutes. $39.95.

Solo Playboating! For solo open canoe paddlers. Filmed on the American, Nantahala, and Gauley Rivers. 1991. 37 minutes. $29.95.

Videos made by Canadian expert canoeist Bill Mason: *Paddle to the Sea; Song of the Paddle; Path of the Paddle: Quiet Water; Path of the Paddle: White Water.* 60 minutes. $19.95.

MAIL-ORDER SOURCES OF EQUIPMENT

BOUNDARY WATERS CATALOG PIRAGIS NORTHWOODS COMPANY

105R North Central Avenue
Ely, MN 55731.
800-223-6565
Full line of gear.
Website: http://www.piragis.com/index.html

CAMPMOR

810 Route 17 North
P.O. Box 999

Paramus, NJ 07652
800-526-4784
Website: http://www.campmor.com/

L. L. BEAN

Casco Street
Freeport, ME 04033
800-221-4221
Website: http://www.llbean.com/

NANTAHALA OUTDOOR CENTER (NOC)

13077 Highway 19 West
Bryson City, NC 28713-9114
800-232-7238
Fax 704-488-8039
Website: http://www.nocweb.com/default.htm Besides a mail order catalog of everything you might want, Nantahala runs custom programs in whitewater instruction and rafting.

NORTHWEST RIVER SUPPLIES, INC.

2009 South Main
Moscow, ID 83843
800-635-5202
Website: http://www.gorp.com/nrs. htm

PADDLE STUFF

1634 South Nevada Street
Oceanside, CA 92054
800-747-6628
Videos, books, etc.

WYOMING RIVER RAIDERS

601 Wyoming Boulevard
Casper, WY 82609
800-247-6068

CANOE MANUFACTURERS

For a full list of manufacturers, see the gear guides published in several of the leading paddling magazines at the end of each year. Here is a partial list.

BEAR CREEK CANOE

RR1, Box 163-B, Route 11
Limerick, ME 04048
207-793-2005

BLUE HOLE CANOE CO.

18079-B James Madison

Highway
Gordonsville, VA 22942
540-832-7855

CHESTNUT CANOE CO.
RR1
Baltimore, Ontario
K0K 1C0 Canada
905-342-3618

DAGGER CANOES & KAYAKS
P.O. Box 1500
Harriman, TN 37748
615-882-0404
Website: http://www.usit.net/hp/
dagger/Dagger2.html

EASY RIDER CANOE & KAYAK
P.O. Box 88108
Seattle, WA 98138
206-228-3633

GREAT CANADIAN CANOES
64 Worcester Providence Turn-
pike
Route 146
Sutton, MA 01590
800-98-CANOE

GRUMMAN CANOES
P.O. Box 549
Marathon, NY 13803
607-849-3211

MAD RIVER CANOE
P.O. Box 610
Waitsfield, VT 05673
800-942-2663
Website: http://www.ecotravel.
com/madriver/

MILLBROOK BOATS
49 Lufkin Road
Weare, NH 03291
603-529-3919

MOHAWK CANOES
963 CR 427 N
Longwood, FL 32750
407-834-3233

OLD TOWN CANOE CO.
58 Middle Street
Old Town, ME 04468
800-595-4400
Website:
http://www.otccanoe.com/
index.htm

PACIFIC CANOE BASE
562 David Street
Victoria, British Columbia
Canada V8T 2C8
604-382-1243

WALDEN PADDLERS
P.O. Box 647
Concord, MA 01742
508-371-3000

WE-NO-NAH CANOE, INC.
P.O. Box 247
Winona, MN 55987
507-454-5430

WESTERN CANOEING
P.O. Box 492
Sumas, WA 98295
604-853-9320

WOODSTRIP WATERCRAFT
1818 Swamp Pike
Gilbertsville, PA 19525
215-326-9282

P H O T O
C R E D I T S

NANCIE BATTAGLIA: 11, 16, 32, 36, 41, 90, 94, 98

PAUL O. BOISVERT: 24, 39, 148 (both)

ERIC EVANS/NEW MEDIA, INC.: 25, 46, 97, 100, 102, 104, 121, 124 (all), 146, 159, 169

JOHN GOODMAN/COURTESY MAD RIVER CANOE: 13, 14-15, 17 (left), 21, 88-89, 89 (both), 101, 111, 113, 122-123 (all), 144

JOHN GOODMAN: 17 (right), 18, 23, 112, 114, 120, 157

GORDON GRANT: 118, 127, 132, 140, 167, 174

BECKY LUIGART-STAYNER: 81, 82, 83

SLIM RAY: 26 (both), 27 (both),109, 130, 133, 135, 138 (both), 151, 153, 160, 171, 173 (both)

DAVID M. DOODY/TOM STACK & ASSOCIATES: 156

CLYDE H. SMITH/PETER ARNOLD, INC.: 142, 178

TERRY WILD STUDIO: 8

GORDON WILTSIE: 19, 37

GEORGE WUERTHNER: 20, 84, 87, 88 (top)

INDEX

25 /